LOCH KIN

THE REV. JOHN GRANT MICHIE

With a new introduction by
Bryn Wayte, Deeside Books, Ballater.

Republished from the enlarged and
revised second edition of 1910.

This edition 2010.

Published by Deeside Books,
18-20 Bridge Street,
Ballater,
Aberdeenshire AB35 5QP
Tel. 01339 754080
Email: deesidebk@aol.com
Web: www.deesidebooks.com

ISBN: 978-1-907813-01-6

Printed and bound by Robertson Printers, Forfar

INTRODUCTION

The Rev. John Grant Michie was a native of Upper Deeside, born at Wester Micras in 1830, a small hamlet on the North Deeside Road between Ballater and Crathie. One of nine children, his early upbringing was characterised by the hard nature of life typical of a crofting community of the period. His very early years were taken up with the herding of their cattle and sheep, and also in taking charge of his two younger brothers. He did not attend school until eight or nine years old, his education up until then having been undertaken by his elder sisters. Despite the family having a poor background they did appear to be quite literate, albeit in the Gaelic language which was predominantly spoken within their home. Thus when Michie first started his formal education he remarked that he felt rather awkward at first among boys who only spoke English - this being the only language that was allowed to be spoken at school.

Michie relates that his desire for reading and learning was initiated by the winning of books as prizes in competitions, and as rewards for merit, during his early school years. From then on the young student entered in to a life of part time study that had to be combined with the necessity of working on the croft in order to contribute towards the family income. In his later teen years he was able to continue his studies through the part time teaching of junior classes to help supplement his meagre resources. This eventually culminated in a position at Ballater school in the winter of 1847-8, which, in return for some teaching of the youngsters,

Michie was to receive private lessons and board and lodgings in the schoolhouse. His ultimate aim was to receive some tuition at Aberdeen Grammar School, and this he succeeded in doing for one term in 1850, and another in the following year. The objective of these sessions was to be coached up for the "Bursary Competition", which would enable entrance to one of the Aberdeen colleges.

Michie succeeded in obtaining a bursary and began his college career in 1851, graduating in 1855. His studies included Latin, Greek, Mathematics and Natural History. It is the latter subject, with the resultant field trips, that inspired an interest in Geology that was to last for the rest of his life. After graduation he was appointed schoolmaster at Logie Coldstone, a post that he held for the next twenty one years. Like many country schoolmasters of those days he kept the possibility of the ministry in mind, and during his early years at Logie Coldstone attended the Divinity classes at Aberdeen University, and became a licentiate of the Church of Scotland. Ministry positions at this time were reliant on patronage and it was not until 1876 that the newly formed parish of Dinnet provided him with a post. Michie was to spend the rest of his life at Dinnet, retiring at the age of 73 due to the infirmities of age, and dying the following year in 1904.

Throughout both his educational and ministerial careers Michie had always had a vibrant interest in both local history and the antiquities of the area, and was exceptional in commiting his findings to paper. His early upbringing within the Gaelic language also gave him access to many of the traditional stories that were handed down by word of mouth, and he was careful to record these. This resulted in his first publication, "Deeside Tales", which appeared in 1872.

The Upper Deeside region has a rich archaeological history and it was well known that the Loch Kinnord area had yielded numerous historical relics to the collector. In 1859 the water level was lowered by drainage operations and some important finds were made. This prompted keen interest from Michie, and the outcome of his studies was the first edition of the "History of Loch Kinnord", published in 1877. The importance of these finds cannot be under-estimated, and this led to Michie communicating with many of the leading historians and archaeoligists of the day.

At this point it would probably be opportune to stand back and review Michie's work in the light of what is known today. Archaeology is a constantly developing science, with new information frequently changing previously held views. Michie was aware of this, and often quotes other authors and their academic publications. This is proved by the fact that Michie was working on this new and revised edition of "Loch Kinnord" prior to his death. To some extent it is highly probable that Michie knew his limitations, and was more than willing to invite other experts to view his finds. Probably one of the most important examples of this is that Michie solicited the help of Sir Alexander Ogston of Glendavan, a near neighbour. Ogston was a renowned Aberdeen surgeon, but also an enthusiastic field-archaeologist in his leisure time. In 1903, at Ogston's suggestion, the Hon. John Abercromby of the Society of Antiquaries supervised a systematic exploration of the area for a period of one month to try to evaluate Michie's findings. Although this was (Page 23) "far too short a time to examine more than a small part of the extensive remains, enough was done to show that they certainly belonged to prehistoric Celtic times." This prompted Ogston to persevere with his quest to obtain additional information, and for the next eight years or so further excavations and surveys were conducted throughout the area by himself and others. All this work was accurately recorded, but it was not until Ogston's death in 1929 that his relatives offered this work to the Third Spalding Club for publication. This culminated in an edited version of Ogston's works appearing under the title of "The Prehistoric Antiquities of the Howe of Cromar" in 1931.

It is important to differentiate between Michie's book and that of Ogston. Michie presents an overview from the prehistoric period through to the Civil War, as well as more recent history and anecdotes about the local area. Ogston, on the other hand, limits himself to the prehistoric period entirely, but presents a much more detailed assessment of the archaeological information known up to that time. My conclusion, therefore, is that "Loch Kinnord" should be thought of more as a local history of the Deeside area rather than an accurate archaeological guide. However, even Ogston's weighty tome has been superseded by more recent knowledge, so everything should be looked at in perspective.

As a dealer in out of print books I have long known that "Loch Kinnord" has been a very difficult item to source. It is therefore the revised and expanded second edition of 1910 that has been reproduced here in its original form, with just some slight variations in pagination due to type sizes. Punctuation, wherever possible, was kept the same so as not to affect the style of writing, and spelling, both in English and Gaelic, are as Michie originally intended.

Although sketch plans and photographs are provided in this second edition no location map was originally included. The majority of the subject area is covered by the modern Ordnance Survey 1:50,000 Landranger Sheet No. 37. However, by far the best maps available are the O.S. Explorer Series at the much larger scale of 1:25,000. This scale is sufficiently large to allow virtually all of the place names identified by Michie to be located, as well as many of the sites of archaeological interest also being shown. Colour contouring also helps for the easy identification of the many hilltop fortifications mentioned. The subject area is predominantly covered by Sheet 405 in this series, with some slight overlap on to Sheet 395.

It is hoped that the reader will enjoy this book for the purpose that it was originally intended - that is, to provide a brief history of the Kinnord (nowadays Kinord) area and some of its more colourful characters. This book may also be read in conjunction with another recent reprint from Deeside Books - "Lochnagar", by Alex Inkson McConnochie. These two books complement each other to provide a coherent understanding of attitudes to, and about, the history of the Upper Deeside area in the Victorian period, when both books were originally conceived. The standard historical reference work for Deeside is generally taken to be "The Royal Valley" by Fenton Wyness published in 1968, and contains an extensive bibliography concerning the area if additional reference material is required. Further advice will be freely given for other books of local interest.

Bryn Wayte,
Deeside Books,
Ballater.
August 2010.
www.deesidebooks.com

LOCH KINNORD

From a water-colour drawing by A. Fraser, Aberdeen

LOCH KINNORD

LOCH KINNORD

ITS HISTORY AND ANTIQUITIES
NEW AND REVISED EDITION
WITH THE CHURCH OF TULLICH
AND OTHER PAPERS ❧ ❧ ❧
BY THE REV. JOHN GRANT MICHIE

WITH 34
ILLUSTRATIONS

ABERDEEN ❧ ❧
D. WYLLIE & SON MCMX

PRINTED BY
WILLIAM SMITH & SONS, THE BON-ACCORD PRESS
ABERDEEN

PREFACE

FROM the favourable reception accorded to the new edition of the late Mr. Michie's *Deeside Tales*, published two years ago, it seems likely that his *History of Loch Kinnord* in a revised and improved form may not be unwelcome. He had himself been planning a second edition more than twenty years ago; but other undertakings having absorbed his time and energies during the later years of his life, this task, laid aside and deferred from time to time, was finally left unaccomplished. It thus remains to his literary executor to give effect to his wishes.

Mr. Michie was the more anxious to see the book in a new edition because he intended to take the opportunity of making certain changes which appeared to him desirable. *Loch Kinnord* was originally published in connection with a local bazaar, and its preparation was in the end somewhat hurriedly completed. Part also of the matter owed its place in the book to the special occasion. Besides, on some of the details his opinion had changed in the light of further consideration and the researches of others in the same field. The new edition was therefore to be recast in some points and revised throughout.

The material which he designed for this purpose was put into the hands of Mr. Francis C. Diack, the editor of *Deeside Tales*, who has adjusted it and prepared the work for the press. He has also added a few articles on some points where fresh information has been forthcoming since the author wrote.

There are also included a few papers by Mr. Michie, cognate in character with the main subject, two of which appear for the first time - "The Church of Tullich" and "Prehistoric Remains at Mulloch." The account of William MacPherson, the local antiquarian "collector" in humble life, appeared in part in the *Aberdeen Free Press*; and for permission to reprint this article I am indebted to the kindness of the editor.

The illustrations, which it is hoped will be both attractive and helpful, would not have been so numerous but for the courtesy of the Council of the Society of Antiquaries of Scotland - of which Mr. Michie was a corresponding member - who obligingly granted the use of the following blocks: plate III, and figs, 1, 4, 5, 8-10, 12-22. The photograph of the bronze spear-head found in Loch Kinnord (fig. 6) is due to the kindness of the late Mr. H. W. Young, of Burghead; and to Mr. Elliot Stock, publisher, London, I am indebted for the use of figs. 2 and 3, from *The Antiquary*.

J. MACPHERSON WATTIE.

BROUGHTY-FERRY, *MAY*, 1910.

CONTENTS

LIST OF ILLUSTRATIONS

PLATES

FIGURES IN TEXT

LIST OF ILLUSTRATIONS

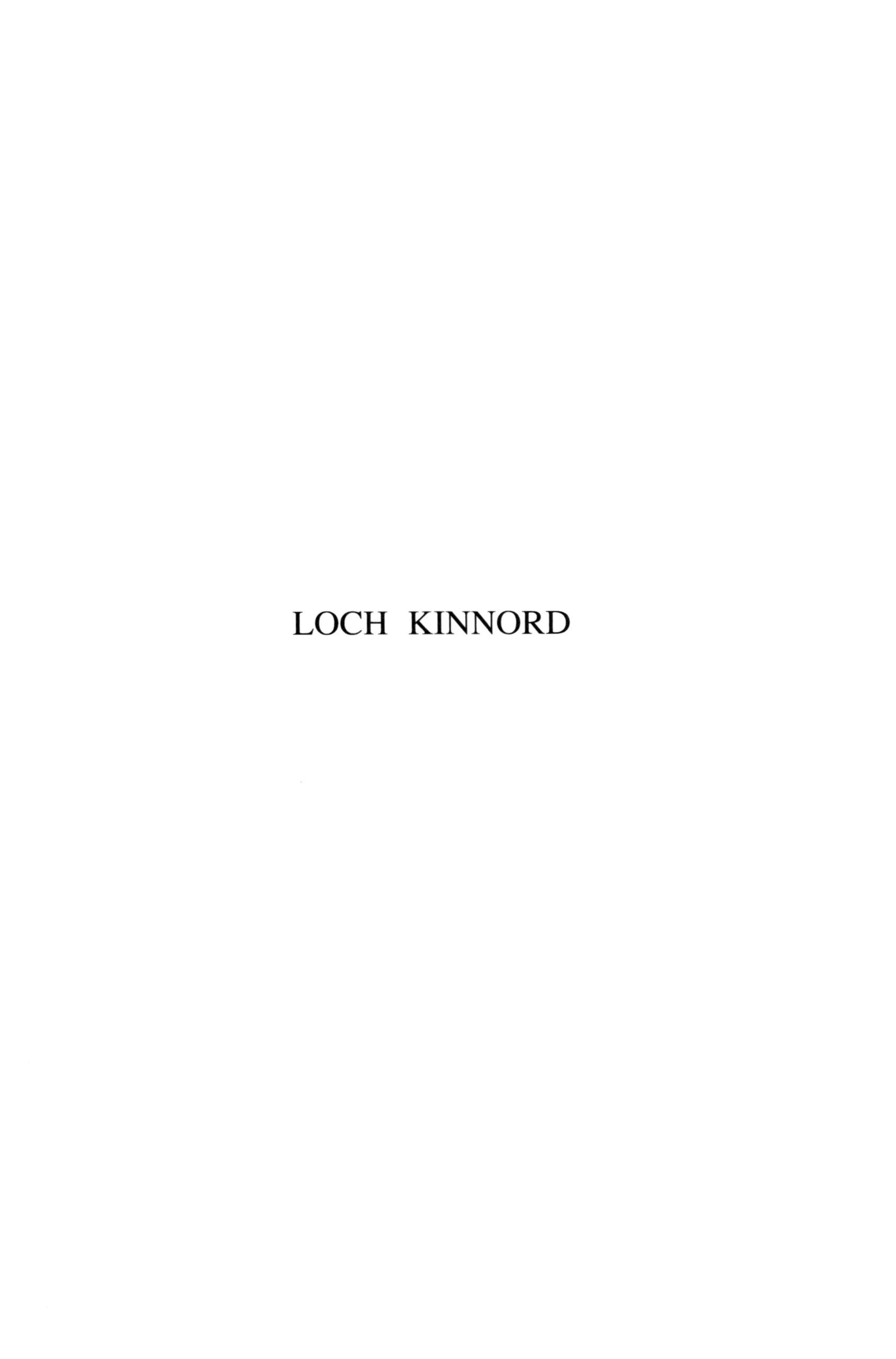

LOCH KINNORD

LOCH KINNORD

CHAPTER I

INTRODUCTORY

LESS than thirty years ago* the upward traveller by the old Deeside coach, on crossing the burn of Dinnet, was apt to fancy himself as entering some vast wilderness of brown heath, where no human habitation had ever stood; and for the next three miles of his journey this impression was likely to be rather strengthened than dissipated by the aspect of the country on either hand. Generally, therefore, it was with a feeling of relief that he found himself wheeled down the somewhat dangerous descent of the narrow old county road, where it swept in alarming proximity to dark Pol Fantrach, from the rocky buttress of Culblean to the door of the roadside hostelry of Cambus o' May. But though concealed from his view, he had all the while been skirting a locality as lovely and picturesque as the moor he had crossed was barren and dreary.

At that time very few strangers were aware of the existence of Loch Kinnord, and fewer still knew

*[Written in 1877].

anything of the charms of its scenery; while the interesting remains of antiquity that abound in the vicinity were but little explored. No one had seen them who could understand their significance or read their story.

Now all this is changed. The new turnpike, opened in 1857, by winding round the northern slope of the Ord, brought the lake and its sylvan environs within view of the passing tourist; but he was content to look at it as at a beautiful scene in a shifting diorama.* There was no convenient place near where he could break his journey and resume it again after a personal examination of the locality. At length, however, the opening of the railway between Aboyne and Ballater (16th October, 1866) gave the desired opportunity. The stations at Dinnet and Cambus o' May afford convenient points from which to reach the lake, whose beautiful shores are now annually visited by crowds of holiday excursionists. Rich in treasures of science and relics of long forgotten ages, it has now become a centre of attraction for naturalists and antiquaries. Some of these relics are of so hoar an antiquity that they throw around the scene something of a hallowed character, suggesting to the intelligent visitor "thoughts of other years," and raising in the imagination pictures of a state of society so remote, that the very outlines of it are but faintly traceable, so far back do they lie in the long vista down which we look into prehistoric times.

*So little was the locality even then known, that in the edition of the Deeside Guide published in 1866, Loch Kinnord and Loch Davan are placed three miles apart, and the line of the Tarland and Ballater road is made to pass between them, whereas they are not 100 yards apart, and the road passes to the north of Loch Davan.

It is with the view of guiding in some measure these thoughts, and throwing, if possible, some light on these pictures that the following brief history of Kinnord is offered to those whose pleasure or curiosity may lead them to visit this interesting district.

CHAPTER II

GEOLOGICAL RECORD

IN speaking of the changes which the face of the country has undergone in the lapse of geological time, I can only advert to those that have occurred within the most recent period - that during which the superficial deposits, the till, the gravel, the sand, the travelled boulders, the moss and the soil were produced, and came to occupy their present positions. If we should seek to go further back than this in quest of information, we should find no resting-place, no record to read, till we had descended to the very earliest ages; for we have in this part of Scotland no intervening deposits between the newest and the oldest. The meaning of this fact, probably, though not certainly, is that never,

> "Since Britain first at Heaven's command
> Arose from out the azure main,"

have these parts been for any considerable length of time, if at all, under the waters of the ocean. Whatever place, therefore, we may take as a people in the history of our race, the country we inhabit will bear comparison, in respect of age with any other on the face of the earth; for in these northern highlands we tread the oldest dry land of the old, old world.

But leaving the long geological cycles that have passed since the first appearance of the crystalline rocks on the dry crust of the earth, we shall begin our short history with the period that immediately preceded the deposition of the till that now mostly overlies them. Just as that period was drawing to a close, the valley of the Dee presented an appearance very different from what it does now. Instead of enclosing a clear continuous stream that collects its principal waters amongst the mountains of Braemar, and flows without interruption over its pebbly or rocky bed to the sea, the valley was then broken up into a series of long, narrow troughs, containing lakes, from the one to the other of which the river leaped over the intervening barriers in grand water-falls or rushed through narrow gorges in wild cataracts. What is now the spur of Culblean was then an intersecting ridge rising on the south into the Bellamore Crag, behind Headinsch. For long ages the lowest point in this rocky barrier was the Slock behind Cambus o' May House, and through this gorge the river, for a great length of time, found its escape from the lake above to the lake below. The tertiary period, to which we are now referring, was not only a warm period, it was in Scotland also one of great earthquakes. There was even a chain of volcanoes on the west coast, pouring out in their frequent eruptions streams of lava, and altering the whole face of the country. It is quite possible that during some of these earthquakes a deeper fissure might have been formed in the ridge of Culblean, to the south of the present channel of the river; and the water might have escaped through it sometime before the close of this period. I have been led to form this conjecture from finding, on an examination of the deposits brought to light by the extensive works carried out round the mansion of Cambus o' May, every nook and crevice in the rocks filled with fine water-wrought sand, evidently carried into these corners by the eddying of the waters. There were sufficient causes in operation during the succeeding epoch to produce this motion in the waters of the lake, and it may have been due to them; but certainly the shifting of the outlet in the manner supposed would have given rise to it, and produced the deposits observed.

At all events, what is now the Moor of Dinnet and the district of Kinnord formed the largest of the whole series of the lakes that there lay in the line of the valley of the Dee. It was produced by a rocky barrier stretching across the valley near Boghead, and uniting the ridge of Balrory on the south with the Mulloch range on the north. Towards the close of this period the passage of the river over this ridge may have been about 100 feet above its present bed. The lake formed by this barrier terminated to the west in a fine bay, the shores of which swept round behind the farm of Balletrach, and stretched northward with many a headland and creek into the district of Cromar, as far at least as the mansion-house of Blelack. At a former period it had been of much greater extent; but the barrier had gradually got worn down by the action of the water, till towards the close of the tertiary age it had shrunk to something like the above dimensions, i.e., about five miles in length from north to south, and three miles of average breadth. Large as it was, it contained but two small islands, situated about a mile-and-a-half apart, near the middle and deepest portion. The roots of these still remain in the rocky

Pl. I.

KINNORD AND DAVAN FROM MULLOCH

eminences of the two heights that bound Loch Kinnord, the one on the north and the other on the south.

Slowly diminishing in size, this lake had continued for countless ages to fill the valley; but a change was now drawing on that was greatly to alter the features of the landscape. From some cause, which has not yet been satisfactorily explained, the climate began to change, and that not for the better. Year by year, or I should rather say, century by century, for the change was slow in its progress, the winter cold became more severe, and the summer heat shorter. The hills, which were then higher and steeper, than they are now, began to wear snowy mantles all the year round; and cold tongues of ice were thrust out from the corries of perpetual snow, and descended a long way down into the valleys beneath. All but the hardiest animals deserted the country. The old forests decayed; and nothing but a scanty arctic vegetation lurked behind, and that only on sheltered and sunny spots in the low grounds. Still, the winter cold went on increasing in severity till every mountain was covered with perpetual snow, and every valley enclosed its glacier. These glaciers stript the country of its former soil, ground it into a fine powder, and, working it up into a soft clay, dropped into its mass the boulders they had torn from the overhanging rocks, and rolled them along often to a great distance. In this manner was formed underneath the glaciers that extensive deposit of stiff clay, studded with stones of all sizes, but mostly somewhat water-rolled, or rather ice-worn, to which geologists give the name of *till.* It generally contained a large quantity of iron, obtained from the decomposed vegetation of the previous era. This element furnished a cement which, when the deposit settled, bound the clay together somewhat like an asphalted floor, and gave rise to the subsoil which agriculturists dread as the most barren and intractable they have to deal with. In this part of the country they call it a pan, which I do not think by any means an inappropriate term. All this went on for many ages, till the whole country was covered with ice and snow - ice-capped, in short, as much of Greenland now is - and the glaciers actually reached the sea. The great glacier that occupied the valley of the Dee was probably at that time not less than a thousand feet thick.

When this had lasted for a period of indeterminable duration, the climate began to get milder; less snow fell in winter, and the summer heat had greater power to melt it. The great ice age was on the wane. But the whole period of its decline was one of fearful floods. The soft snows on the surface melted first; and the old valleys being blocked up with hard glacial ice, the streams reeled along in directions often the very reverse of what they now take. And though their courses were over the ice, they carried along quite as much sand and stones as if they had run in channels of ordinary soil; for these decaying glaciers were covered to a great depth with the rock *debris* that had been accumulating on them for ages. They are sometimes found in this condition still among the Himalayas, so that travellers can scarcely tell whether they be walking on firm ground or on *debris*-covered glaciers. It is this circumstance that has mostly given rise to the difficulty of understanding how mounds of water-borne materials could have been collected in the unlikely situations in which they occur.

At length all the snow and smaller glaciers had shrunk

back to the higher hills, but the great glaciers still continued, though in diminished bulk, to fill the main valleys, and obstruct the natural drainage of the country. The Dee glacier, hundreds of feet in thickness, formed a dam at Dinnet so deep that the lake behind it stretched back to the skirts of Morven. Meantime the wear and tear which the face of nature was undergoing was not less during the decay than during the prevalence of the ice age, though the agent and the kind of work done were different. At first it was rivers of ice, now it was headlong floods of water; and between them they produced such a transformation of hill and dale, that if one could have seen the country before and after, he could scarcely have known it to be the same. The very hills were different. In most instances their summits were flattened, their sides sloped, and their corries changed. They were, indeed, only the weather-beaten stumps of what they had once been; while the old lakes that had lain in the valleys below were almost all gone, and their beds occupied by unsightly wastes of water-rolled stones and sand, as bare as fresh river *stanners*. This, at least, was the result in the case of the Moor of Dinnet. Remnants of the former lake, it is true, still survived in straggling patches. But the great ice river had worn away the rocky barrier, and only in the deeper depressions of the old bottom, as at Kinnord, Davan, and the Ordie Moss, was there any water remaining that could properly be called a lake.

Kinnord was a most unlovely place then, with the Dee almost on a level with its lake, coursing in scattered streams round shingly islands here and there. At last, however, it gathered its waters together, and by slow degrees scooped out for itself its present channel. While it was so occupied, and it must have taken a long time to do it, vegetation, under the improving climate, was busy clothing the face of nature. The shallower pools were becoming swamps and morasses; every plant was taking root in its suitable habitat, and every tree in its friendly soil. The animal tribes, also, to whose habits the country and climate were favourable, were gradually finding their way back into the unoccupied territory.

When things had arrived at this pass, the Geological record may be said to have closed; and we next open the Prehistoric Volume.

CHAPTER III

PREHISTORIC PERIOD

WE have now to deal with the appearance of man upon the scene, though when or whence he came we know not. A few thousand years more or less are of no consequence in fixing a date so remote.

The first human inhabitants of this part of Aberdeenshire probably came from the south. They were in a very savage condition, and had enough to do to maintain their ground against the attacks of the wild beasts of the forest without making war on each other. They had no knowledge of any art save hunting and fishing; and they have left behind them no record of their manner of life, except a few rude stone cups and chips of hard rock which served their simple wants and supplied to them the place of dishes and knives. These are now rarely met with in the district around Kinnord.

Another race, somewhat more civilized, but belonging to the same Celtic stock, crossed the Grampians and settled on Deeside, making slaves of the former inhabitants, or driving them back into the remoter glens. After some ages these were in like manner dispossessed by some other tribe, hailing also from the south. It was the old story over again, as recorded in Deuteronomy, "As he did to the children of Esau which dwelt in Seir, when He destroyed the Horims from before them; and they succeeded them and dwelt in their stead even unto this day; and the Avims which dwelt in Hazerim even unto Azzah, the Caphtorims, which came forth out of Caphtor, destroyed them and dwelt in their stead."

Each victorious tribe or race was, however, more civilized than its predecessor; and thus a knowledge of one art after another found its way into the district. Each succeeding tribe was also more powerful in numbers than the one it had dispossessed, and required wider land to support it. These circumstances gave rise to wars between neighbouring tribes, which were at first carried on with the simplest weapons that nature supplied, namely clubs and stones. The conflicts they thus engaged in were not an unmixed evil; for the love of mastery, which is one of the strongest passions in the savage mind, supplied a continual and strong stimulus to the contending tribes to invent some more effective engine of destruction than that possessed by their enemies. This set their intellects a-working, and tended greatly to promote the progress of art in other and more peaceful departments. Battle stones - round stones attached to the wrist by means of long thongs of skin, which could be thrown at the head of an enemy and then jerked back by the string - are among the earliest manufactured weapons found in the district. To the invention of battle stones succeeded that of slings; to the slings stone darts; and to the stone darts, bows and arrows. Relics of all these are found, though rarely, in the soils and morasses around Kinnord, and testify to the sanguinary struggle for possession then going on.

Meantime much improvement had taken place in the

arts of peace. The old rude stone cup had been superseded by an ornamental article furnished with a handle; and the rough chip that did duty for a knife was going out of fashion, and regularly-shaped flints were coming into use instead; while for heavier work stone axes and hammers were being fabricated. About this time also the purchase power of the lever was discovered; and not long after, an ingenious practical application of the principle was made, by attaching levers or handles to the hammers and axes which had formerly been held in the hand. This was an immense stride onwards in the progress of art, even though at first the handle was attached to the head by means of thongs of skin. The art of boring circular holes, not only in timber but in stone also, followed soon after, and then the handle was inserted into a hole or socket in the head itself. Several such implements have been found, if not in the immediate neighbourhood of Kinnord, at least within the district of Cromar.

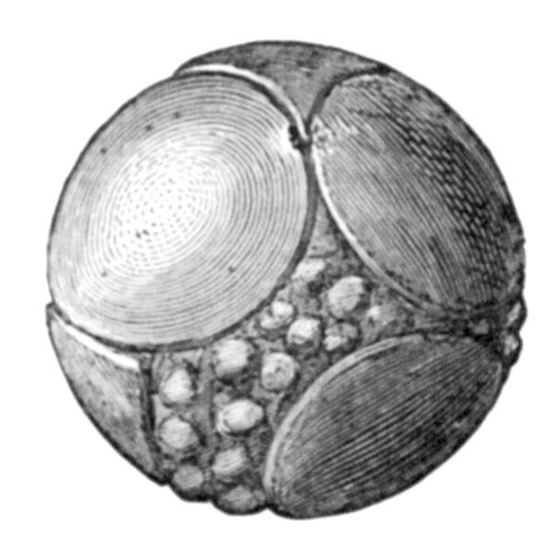

FIG. I. - ORNAMENT STONE BALL FOUND
BESIDE STONE CIST NEAR BALLATER
(Diameter 2 7/8 in.)

But of all improvements in the arts that were effected at this early stage, none was so important as that of polishing stone. The man who discovered this was in his day and generation almost as great a benefactor of his species as he who invented the steam-engine. From the period when men learned to polish their stone tools may be dated the rise of all handicraft. An edge could thus be obtained on stone which for keenness was not surpassed for long after the introduction of metal implements. This improvement, however, does not seem to have been taken much advantage of so far north as Kinnord, till shortly before the bronze age; for very few specimens of polished stone belonging to this early age are now found in the district.

To these simple stone tools were afterwards added bronze ones; and, before the stage of civilization to which I am referring had come to a close, some little aid was also obtained from iron, though it was doubtless a very rare commodity at that time.

Such being the tools of the early inhabitants, let us now see what they were able to accomplish with them. They felled the trees of the forest, which they converted into canoes, implements of husbandry, and other tools, with which they rolled together great stones for walls of defence. With the means at their command, they built great circular houses above ground, and strange pear-shaped ones under. In short, they contrived to make themselves almost comfortable and secure; and when we consider what they achieved, it cannot be said that they were indolent, and did not make the most of their means.

There is reason to believe that the settlement at

Kinnord, leading such an existence as I have described, was one of the earliest and most populous north of the Grampians. The locality had, indeed, unusual attractions, possessing, as it did, the natural elements of security against enemies from without, and of food supply for the dwellers within. Naturally the earliest settlers would select for their residence a locality where the necessaries of life could be obtained in the greatest abundance, and with the least toil; and of these wood and water must have been the most essential. Both were here to be found in unusual store. Timber for the construction of their dwellings, and for fuel to warm them, was at hand; while the lakes and the forest would afford an unfailing supply of food. Irrespective, therefore, of the remains of antiquity which have been found in the district, there was a presumption in the very character of its situation that it must early have attracted attention as a place peculiarly favourable for a settlement.

In these very olden times the idea of a town, as known to us, had not been conceived. A town then embraced a little district, selected in the first instance for its natural facilities of defence, and afterwards fortified by art so as to afford protection, not only to the inhabitants, but to all their flocks and herds. The Romans were the first to describe these ancient British towns; and from their accounts we gather that they were generally situated in woods, in localities where lakes and marshes were abundant and formed natural defences against invasion. In these lakes the natives built artificial islands, and palisaded those that nature had built, in order to render them safe retreats in case of defeat from an invading foe.

The lake-dwellers spent most of their time on the

water - an element with which they had acquired great familiarity. Their aquatic feats much surprised the Romans, who at first took them for a sort of amphibious race of the human family, and believed they scarcely could be drowned.

But besides the water and marsh defences, they were also very fond of building *hill-forts*, where the nature of the country afforded them facilities for so doing. The most prominent heights were selected for fortifications, and around these clustered the rude huts of the people; just as in more recent times every castle was surrounded by a hamlet to which it afforded protection against assaults from foreign enemies. A collection of these hill-forts and lake retreats, occupied by the same people, and capable from their situations of affording help to each other, though scattered over a pretty wide extent of country, was in these early days esteemed a town.

Now the remains which still survive (and some account of which will be given in the course of the work) are sufficient to show that the country all around Kinnord was the headquarters of some great tribe. The district thus formed into a town embraced the whole valley of the Burn of Dinnet, with probably a portion of that of the Burn of Tarland; but the principal strength, or chief citadel, was in and around the two lochs. The town was not known by the name Kinnord; if the people used that word at their first settlement, they applied it to only a small portion of their fortified district - a portion which afterwards became important as it rose by degrees to be the principal fortress. The name which the inhabitants themselves bestowed on the city was Davan, or the land or town of *the two lakes*, a name which it must be allowed was, and even yet is, very descriptive of the situation; for these two lakes, now called Davan and Kinnord, though greatly modified in shape and extent from what they then were, still form the principal feature of the scenery. From this circumstance, then, they called their town Davan, or the *Town of the Two Lakes*.

Possessing such an advantageous situation for their capital, they in time succeeded in bringing under subjection their less favoured neighbours, till at length their territories probably extended over the whole valleys of the Dee and Don, and, as some think, along the sea coast from the mouths of these rivers almost to where Peterhead now stands.

It may be thought that the town of Davan, as we shall now call it, did not occupy a very central position for being the chief town of such a people; but it must be recollected that they did not then select sites for their cities in the most central localities, but at first for purposes of defence, and long after for those of commerce. Even so late, comparatively, as when chief towns were chosen for counties, little regard was paid to central situation, as may be seen from the selection of Aberdeen, Banff, and many others of the county towns of Scotland. In the much earlier times to which we are referring, the natural defences of mountain and flood were of more consequence.

CHAPTER IV

PREHISTORIC PERIOD

TO 1000 A.D.

PERHAPS it may be asked, if there was such a very great town here, ought we not to find more extensive ruins of it than the district now exhibits? But we have to remember that the structures raised by a rude people are peculiarly liable to become obliterated. Their common dwellings were mere huts, generally of turf or timber, and even their stone buildings were uncemented by lime or mortar, and readily fell into shapeless ruins, while the materials of which they were composed, being selected stones, were much valued by the modern mason and dyker, and consequently carried away in great quantities for the construction of neighbouring houses and dry-stone walls. Add to this that the very sites of many of these old habitations must have disappeared in the course of the reclaiming of waste lands which modern farmers have carried on so vigorously, and little surprise need be felt that not more of these ruins still survive to mark the site of this prehistoric city. More, however, are still extant than the casual visitor may fancy. Let us examine the neighbourhood of the two lochs with some degree of minuteness.

Between Kinnord and Davan there rises to the height of

100 feet above the water level the elevated ridge now called the Wood of Kinnord, showing a pretty bold and wooded front towards Loch Kinnord on the south, but sloping more gradually to the shore of Loch Davan on the north. The surface is very rough, being thickly strewn with large erratic boulders of granite with here and there a rugged outcrop of the underlying rock. Notwithstanding its roughness, a portion of the north-western slope has been brought under cultivation; and all traces of ancient remains that may have existed there have been effaced. The same remark applies to the south-eastern slope, but the rest of the ground remains in its natural condition. Protected by its ruggedness, and by the growth of natural wood, no disturbance of the surface, and no erections save the farm-steadings and stone dykes enclosing the arable land have been made for a very long period, so that the modern are easily distinguished from the ancient ruins. Those that are modern are quite modern, and the ancient are very ancient. Yet it was not till the year 1857 that the vestiges of ancient dwellings which this ridge contains came under the notice of any person competent to judge of their character. It is true they were well enough known to the tenants around Kinnord, among whom they had long excited some curiosity to know something of their origin. Tradition being dark on the subject, superstition, as usually happens in such circumstances, was had recourse to in order to solve the mystery of their history, and their erection was ascribed to supernatural agency. In the year above noted Dr. Joseph Robertson, the eminent antiquary, during a visit to Cromar, heard of the "Fairy Faulds"; and judging, from his great knowledge of country people's modes of

thought, that the supernatural here meant the very ancient, he resolved and found means to be conducted to them. Once on the ground he discovered several circular foundations besides those known to his guide, and traced the circumvallation of the whole cluster. I have been told by the late Rev. Mr. Wattie, Bellastraid, that Dr. Robertson unhesitatingly pronounced the ruins to be the remains of a Pictish village. This cluster, which we may call group I, is east of Old Kinnord, not far from the south shore of Loch Davan. In 1859 I made a careful examination of the whole height, called Wood of Kinnord, in the course of which I alighted on another group (II), which lies immediately north of the farm-steading of New Kinnord. Some years afterwards my attention was called to certain statements in the New Statistical Account of the Parish of Aboyne, written by the minister in 1842, in which mention is made of similar ruined foundations on the neighbouring hills of Mulloch and Knockice, and also of "two parallel dykes, forming a fenced avenue or roadway," leading westwards in the direction of Kinnord. Guided by this, I went over the ground indicated, but could find only faint traces of the walled road. Beginning on the hill of Knockice, one mile east of Kinnord, I followed such marks as I could find over the moorish shoulder on to the flat below, where I could find no trace of it. Continuing, however, to go forward in the direction indicated, I was enabled to find it again after crossing the flat. Here it was much better marked than on any part of Knockice, and following it for 300 yards from its first re-appearance, I was unexpectedly conducted to a third group (III) of circular foundations, north-east of New Kinnord. Beyond this, the road took the direction of some arable fields, and could not be further traced.

To return to group I. This consists of ten traceable foundations of a circular form, two distinct walled approaches, and a complete line of circumvallation, besides other ruins, the forms of which cannot now be defined. The entire length of the surrounding wall, exclusive of the portion forming the entrance passages, is 625 yards. It appears to have been of small elevation; and judging from the ruins that remain - not always a safe criterion - could scarcely have been intended for defence. The entrance passage leading north-west is deeply sunk in the ground, and sweeps round an eminence abrupt on all sides, except that sloping towards the passage. No marks of ruins appear on this height. The summit is within easy stone-cast of this passage, which, judging from its width and depth, formed the principal entrance from the west; indeed, leading as it did towards the narrow isthmus between the two lakes, it formed the only entrance in this direction. The other entrance, or walled passage, which is straight, leads off south-west in the direction of the Claggans. It is also commanded by an eminence, which however is enclosed within the line of circumvallation and contains traces of ruins; and on its summit there is an upright stone, standing 4 feet above ground. Except in three cases, the entrances into the circular enclosures cannot be traced owing to the demolition of the walls, and in two of these it is doubtful whether what appears to be the entrances are not gaps in the walls, made subsequently to their becoming ruins. In some the stones are of moderate size, in others there are very heavy blocks. The interiors are sunk to some depth below the level of the natural surface. The most conspicuous of these is the only one which appears to have had its floor paved. The pavement, composed of slabs of granite, is still almost entire, and is laid together with some skill.

Group II contains six well defined foundations, together with a labyrinth of ruins, of which it is impossible to make out the forms owing to the complete demolition of the walls. As in group I, the centre enclosure is the deepest, has the highest walls, and appears to have been the chief dwelling. The whole area embraced in these enclosures is commanded by a conical height surrounded by a stone rampart. It contains numerous traces of ruins, but of no definite shape. Between groups II and III the ground has been much searched for building stones, and whatever ruins there may have been there have been obliterated. It is highly probable, however, that they formed but one cluster of structures covering the whole space.

Group III was by far the largest, and, in the condition in which I first examined it, presented the appearance of a regular town on a small scale, with one main street running through it and several others branching off to either hand. About the year 1885, however, these stones attracted the attention of the road-menders, and many of them were broken up for road-metal, so that, though there are heaps of stones remaining, the plan and outlines of the ruins as originally noticed are now obliterated. The whole area embraced by the two groups in the neighbourhood of New Kinnord cannot be less than 15 acres, but as they border on arable land, it is impossible to fix limits to the space they may have occupied. That this was a very considerable place, and for its time accommodated a large population,

Pl. II.

LOCH KINNORD FROM THE ORD

there can scarcely be a doubt. No lime or mortar of any kind has been discovered in any of these walls. In all the groups there are certain pear-shaped enclosures, reminding one of the forms of "eirde houses." These generally lie close along the outside of some circular wall, with the interior of which they may have had some communication.*

Leaving now the shores of the loch, let the visitor plant himself on the summit of the Ord, and restore in imagination the hill forts whose foundations and ruins are still traceable within view of his position, each with its attendant outworks and hamlet, and a feeling of astonishment at their number and magnitude, rather

[*The antiquarian visitors whom Mr. Michie was in the way of taking to inspect these remains sometimes found it difficult to see them with quite the same eye as their cicerone. His Pictish buildings might equally well be, it was sometimes held, the handiwork of modern or at least mediaeval times; and in the absence of direct proof one way or another, this view of their origin was perhaps as generally received as the Pictish. The circular enclosures were frequently dismissed as disused sheep-folds. The only way of settling the matter was by recourse to the pickaxe and shovel, but it does not appear that excavations were ever attempted. In 1903, however, at the suggestion of Mr. Ogston of Glen Davan, the Hon. John Abercromby, of the Society of Antiquaries, superintended a systematic exploration. A month was found far too short a time to examine more than a small part of the extensive remains, but enough was done to show that they certainly belong to prehistoric Celtic times. The decisive proof is that two underground or "Picts" houses came to light in the course of the investigations. Some account of the discoveries will be found in the Note on "The Islands" at the end.]

than one of disappointment that so few remain, is likely to fill his mind. If these old ruins were restored to their pristine forms, beginning at the upper end of the valley on

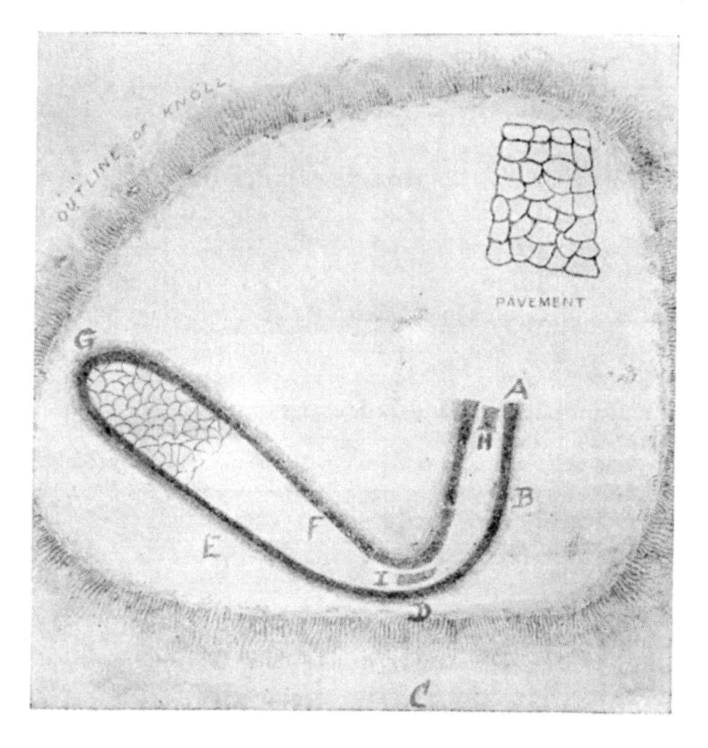

FIG. 2. - GROUND PLAN OF EARTH-HOUSE AT MILTON OF WHITEHOUSE (NEAR BLUE CAIRN)

the slopes of Morven, his eye might discern in the distance three clusters of buildings, with a round tower in each, and a great central tower, the ruins of which are now known as the Blue Cairn, overtopping the others, and forming a conspicuous object on the mountain side. As he carries his eye round the head of the valley, clusters of buildings and smaller towers meet his view in close succession, till it is arrested by an immense pile on the summit of Knocksoul, the most commanding eminence in this direction. A

FIG. 3. - EARTH-HOUSE: VIEW AT D.
(SEE PLAN OPPOSITE)

smaller tower on a humbler knoll to the east is succeeded on the next eminence by the great fort on this side, whose ruins were long known as Cairnmore, or *great cairn* though nothing but the name and the faint outline of the surrounding trench now remains.*

*From these ruins a farm-steading, a hamlet, and several miles of stone dykes were built before the foundations, still of great extent, were cleared away, and the site converted into arable land.

Other two knolls, rising at short intervals towards the south-east are also crowned with forts and encircled with numerous dwellings. Then follows a hollow containing a lake, but hid from view by an elevated ridge called Licklies hill, which has three forts on prominent points, and bristles with other buildings which continue in an easterly direction till another massive pile meets the view, the remains of which are also called Cairnmore. All round these remains almost every rood of uncultivated ground contains the outlines of ancient circular foundations. Carrying the eye still eastward, over the more elevated ridge of the Whitehill, other two towers appear, crowning its chief summits, while almost in line with the more easterly, but farther to the south, and nearer the beholder, the Knockhill and its two neighbouring heights have each its strength, while here, even more densely and extensively than at Cairnmore, are the foundations of other structures traceable. The highest summit in this direction is Knockargetty. Here the situation was defended by three concentric lines of circumvallation, flanked right and left by two strong forts on either hand, the ruins of which still remain in the cairns at Leys and the blue cairns of Ruthven, while the rear was guarded by a line, of forts, not however within view, crowning the Drummy ridge towards the north-east. Carrying the eye still farther southward, it is next arrested by the huge pile that crowns the summit of the Mulloch hill, and the view being now nearer, a whole colony, or suburban town, is discernible around the Loch of Braeroddach, and the heights, seven in number, that bound it in a semicircle, are seen to be surmounted by strong forts, communicating with each other and with the numerous hamlets on the slopes below them by means of walled roadways, and these again similarly connected with the central district between Lochs Davan and Kinnord. To the south of Knockice the knoll called Tomachaillich, overlooking the valley of the Dee, is surmounted by a strong fort and encumbered with lesser structures. Casting the eye now along the slopes to the south of the Dee, the attention is attracted by another fortress and its defences. This is now called Tillycairn; and, judging from the numerous cairns still visible there, and the bronze weapons and other relics of antiquity that have from time to time been found in these ruins, it must have been an extensive and important settlement. Doubtless the Dee flowed between it and the central strength at Kinnord, but there was a good ford in the river, with a fort in the neighbourhood, as is evident from the name *Dinnet*, the first syllable of which is *dun*, a fort. When so many canoes, great and small, were plying on the lakes, it is but reasonable to think that there was also abundant means for crossing the river at seasons when the ford could not be taken. For this purpose, as well as for the sake of the fishings, there can be no doubt that the large boat-pool of Dinnet had a fleet of craft suitable for the trade there carried on. Let our supposed beholder now turn his attention in the direction of the slopes of Culblean to the north-west, and he may discern in the midst of the dense forest that covered its base and sides, two, if not more, populous settlements, each with its protecting forts. One of these extends from the Burn of the Vat northwards to the shores of Loch Davan, the other is still farther north on the slopes of the Lump of Culblean.

The valley is thus seen to be encircled with forts and outposts, great and small, each having its hamlet of more or less importance. The bottom of the hollow so encircled was occupied by mosses, marshes, lochs, and dense thickets of alder, birch, and willow - the principal hunting-ground of the inhabitants, where the wild boar and his family found their winter retreat, and the deer and the wild cattle devoured the rank vegetation.

But the strongest position of all is in and around the two lakes. The beholder we have supposed as surveying this scene might fancy himself seated on the dry-stone battlements of the fort that crowned the Ord; at his feet and around the slopes on all sides are the circular huts and enclosures of the natives, while on the lake, of which his position commands a bird's-eye view, there are vessels of many kinds and sizes, from the great "man of war" canoe 30 feet long, hollowed out of a single oak, with its full complement of marines, to the little skiff with its single rower. On its surface appear two islands, the larger natural but strongly palisaded round and round, and forming an impregnable strength in any mode of warfare then known; the other wholly artificial, and raised by an immense expenditure of labour, doubtless to give increased accommodation and security as the city grew in importance and population.* Besides these two islands, which might be called the inner citadels of the town, a great peninsula, now called *Gardiebane* was also converted into an island-strength by means of a large canal cut across the narrow isthmus. The access was protected on the inside

[*See Chapter IX and Note on "The Islands" at the end.]

by a rampart, and on the land side by heavy stone works, the foundations of which were discovered some years ago. Near the summit of the Wood of Kinnord, on the opposite side of the lake, there is another building - whether a fort or not is not certain - and on the shores of Loch Davan, there are the clusters of hamlets which we have already referred to, as well as those at the eastern end of the Wood of Kinnord. This populous part is seen to be connected with the outlying settlement at Knockice by the roadway already mentioned, which continues its course to the shores of Loch Kinnord opposite the artificial island.

The above description of the great Pictish settlement at Davan is doubtless imaginary; but in filling up the picture not a single detail has been gratuitously assumed; the buildings have only been raised upon ruins or remains that are still visible; of hundreds of others that beyond doubt have been wholly obliterated by the improvements of the modern agriculturist, no account has been taken. But if we restore only those buildings of which the traces and foundations still remain, it is impossible not to see that in some prehistoric age there must have been a strongly fortified centre of a large and busy population - in short, a great ancient city.

How long it remained so it would be rash to conjecture; but there are not wanting evidences that it was visited by the hostile Roman legions, probably those under the command of the Emperor Severus (208 A.D.). These Romans certainly about this period passed near to the city of Davan, which, according to a custom of theirs, they latinized into Davana, or Devana. Whether the Romans completely defeated the inhabitants, and utterly destroyed their city of Devana, we have no means of ascertaining for certain, but that the town received a crushing blow from them there is every reason to believe. That they even made themselves masters of it is almost beyond a doubt, and there is still current a tradition that a great battle was fought between the Britons and the Romans near Knockice. On the whole, the probability is that after being captured by these victorious foreigners, the town never regained its former importance, but gradually sank into decay.*

A long, long night of darkness and silence now overshadowed Kinnord, broken only by a little star-light gleam that shone through the gloom when the Christian religion was introduced among this ancient people. What share they had in the conflicts with the conquering Scots, who came from Ireland into Scotland, much as the Normans long after came from France into England, with

*As to the site of the ancient city of Devana, the learned and accurate antiquary and historian, William F. Skene, LL.D., in his "Celtic Scotland" - Vol. 1, p. 74 - writes:- "Farther north along the coast, and reaching from the mountain chain of the Mounth to the Moray Firth, were the 'Taexali,' who gave their name to the headland now called Kinnaird's Head. Their town, Devana, is placed by Ptolemy in the Strath of the Dee, near the Pass of Ballater, and close to Loch Daven, where the remains of a native town are still to be seen, and in which the name of Devana seems yet to be preserved." In a foot-note on the same page he adds:- "All editions (*i.e.*, of Ptolemy) agree in placing Devana in the interior of the country at a distance of at least thirty miles from the coast. Its identity with the seaport of Aberdeen rests upon the authority of Richard of Cirencester alone."

The conclusion, therefore, that the ancient Devana of the Romans was situated within the district of Loch Kinnord, is one which, on quite a different line of evidence from that followed in the present work, has the support of very high authority on such matters.

Pl. III.

THE KINNORD STONE

the view of establishing themselves as the aristocracy of the country, we have no certain intelligence; we only know that if they came into collision the Picts, or at least the Pictish language, must have ultimately gone down before the more civilized invaders.

Sometime between the years 550 and 600 A.D. the Christian religion was first preached to the natives. The new religion, by obliterating all traces of the ancient idolatry, did much to accelerate the decay of any lingering tradition of heathenish greatness that might still be clinging to their memories. One mode which the disciples of Columba adopted to effect this purpose was to seize possession of the sacred places as sites for the Christian churches they planted. This they in all probability did at Kinnord, though direct evidence is not forthcoming. We can, however, point to the site of one of the earliest Christian establishments in the district. On the north side of the loch, opposite the larger island, at a spot called the Claggans, stood a great stone on which is carved a curiously wrought cross (see plate III), the emblem of the new faith. The style and workmanship of the design are those of the early centuries of the Celtic Church. This stone may now be seen within the policies of Aboyne Castle, whither it was removed for greater security and more careful preservation. On the flat where it originally stood there are still traceable several vestiges of circular foundations (three quite distinct), formed of large stones set on end. They each enclose a space of from 9 to 12 ft. in diameter, and are evidently only a part of a much larger cluster now wholly obliterated by the tillage of the adjoining ground. There are still traditions of a chapel in the immediate neighbourhood.

With the exception of this little star-light glimpse - by means of which we get a momentary glance, dim enough, of an important ecclesiastical change - the long night of silence and darkness remains unbroken for 500 years more. During these long ages the old ruins got hoary, moss-covered, and grey. The people could not understand what they were the relics of, but concluded they must contain treasure; thus many of them were rifled again and again, and turned into shapeless cairns, in which condition they have ever since remained, unless when the mason and stone-dyker have pillaged them for the erection of modern works.

We have now reached what may be called the close of the prehistoric record; and when the light again appears all the old grandeur of Davan and Kinnord was completely forgotten. Need we be surprised then that, after 800 years of desolation and oblivion of the past, so few relics should remain of this ancient city? It required the practised eye of an antiquarian traveller to discover in the green mounds on the banks of the Tigris the ruins of the ancient palaces of Nineveh. Of the most populous region of the kingdom of Israel, a recent traveller remarks:- "Nature has resumed her quiet reign over the hill of Jezreel. All is silent and desolate now; Baal and his worshippers have passed away, and so have the calves of Bethel and of Dan, and the very memory of these events and their actions has departed from the land. There are only two boats now on the sea of Galilee; there is no town now on its shores, and no ruin save the scattered brick pavements of ancient Tiberias. Yet this lake was in our Saviour's days one of the busiest scenes in Palestine, with a dozen or more flourishing towns on its shores, gay palaces giving to it the air of wealth and splendour, and a thriving traffic enlivening its waters."* When we reflect that these towns and palaces were structures raised with the highest arts of architecture, while the round towers of ancient Devana were the rudest efforts of that art, the wonder is not that so few, but that so many, relics of its former greatness should still survive.

*Dr. M'Leod.

CHAPTER V

EARLY HISTORIC PERIOD

TO 1335 A.D.

ERE this period opens on Kinnord, many important political changes had taken place in the history of the country. The different provinces, long petty independent kingdoms, had, one after another, been incorporated into a united nation. The invasions of the Danes, though mostly confined to the coast, had been heard of far inland, and the reports of their deeds of arms, their savage cruelties and sacrileges, had filled the native mind with fear and horror, and given rise to fables that attributed every ruin and trace of devastation to these pirates; and hence arose, as far as I can conjecture, the elements of the tradition that referred to the Danish wars the great cairns and ruins to be found on the bleak moors and hill tops around Loch Kinnord. But the times of the Danes had also passed away, and other disturbers of the country's peace had put them almost out of people's memories.

When these events had come and gone, a great revolution, with which I think Kinnord was associated, swept over the land. In the year 1039, King Duncan, "the Generous," was murdered by one of his great lords, or thanes, of the name of Macbeth. When this Macbeth, who was a descendant of the ancient Pictish kings, got full possession of the kingdom, he resorted to the old

Pictish practice of having round forts on the hill tops, and inaccessible strengths in the marshes and lakes. He built a great round fortress on the top of the hill of Dunsinane, and restored others in different parts of his dominions, such as at Lumphanan, Strathbogie, and I think it very likely on the island at Kinnord also, because he was fond of such strengths, and resided much in this part of his territories. Macbeth was a sort of Oliver Cromwell in his day, and was a good king for the country, though very cruel to the late king's family and followers, all of whom he killed that he could lay his hands on. However, Malcolm, the eldest son, managed to escape into England, whence he returned after seventeen years, accompanied with a great army, gave battle to Macbeth at his great fort of Dunsinane, beat him, and chased him north over the hills to the Peel-Bog in Lumphanan. Here the fugitive made another stand; but Macduff, Malcolm's chief general, overcame him, slew him with his own hand, and carried his head in triumph to the King, who was staying at Kincardine O'Neil. This was that Malcolm who was nicknamed Canmore, or the *Big-headed*, because, as I suppose, he had a large head, perhaps also because he was a very shrewd and wise king. Being now crowned king, he took possession of all the strongholds which Macbeth had built or fortified, Kinnord doubtless among the others, and likely enough garrisoned them with his own soldiers.

That Malcolm Canmore was in the habit of visiting and residing on Deeside seems the only possible explanation of the plentiful store of legends - some of them of old standing, I believe - which are, or at least were, current regarding him. Not many years ago they were constantly repeated all over the district among the "forenicht" fireside stories. The same is true of Braemar, his head-quarters there, according to tradition, being the Castle of Kindrochit. Tradition generally deals with the mythical period of a people's history and ceases when written records begin to be made. It has not been so with this district, where the Celtic habit of passing on from generation to generation "the tales of other years" survived in full force almost till the present day. Naturally, changes and embellishments are introduced on the original historical event till it is often disguised out of all recognition, but below the most extravagant tale there is generally some solid substratum of fact. The legends concerning Malcolm record that he had a palace on the larger island and a prison on the smaller; that he spent much of his time in this royal residence administering the affairs of the nation and enjoying the pleasures of the chase of which he was very fond. To these general facts are added a large number of minute details regarding both his public and private life, such as, that one day on returning from the forest after a successful hunt, he indulged in a little boasting, a weakness to which he was said to be considerably addicted; that his queen, who is represented as anything but an angel in temper, took her royal consort sharply to task for his vanity. An altercation took place, Malcolm rudely telling her that he would do as much by her kith of Denmark as he had done to the game he had that day bagged, in token whereof he dangled a ptarmigan before her face. She, on her part, far from being terrified by his threatening countenance and manner, dared him to repeat the words he had used to her, a defenceless woman, in the hearing of her people. He retorted that he would do so at her brother's court; and to make good his word he soon after set out for Denmark, attended by twelve of his staunchest followers, each armed with a dagger concealed in his sleeve. While he and his attendants were being hospitably entertained to dinner by his brother-in-law, Malcolm did repeat the challenged words; and his followers made good his retreat by each stabbing the two Danes who sat nearest him at table. This treacherous affair led to a war between the two countries, in which the Danes, encouraged by some trifling successes, sent an army to lay siege to the fortress of Kinnord in which the king then resided, and where he had collected the few forces he had been able to draw together. After a good deal of skirmishing (the details of which are unimportant and variously related) on different parts of the Moor of Dinnet, where the cairns underneath which the slain were buried may still be seen, both armies prepared for the decisive conflict. The battle took place on a Monday (hence Munandawan = Monday o' the dawin!) and the Danes, though numbering four to one, were signally defeated, mainly in consequence of twelve Argyllshire men approaching the scene of action at the critical moment, each carrying a flag and blowing a bagpipe. The Danes, mistaking this for a new army, immediately took to flight along the ridge of hills leading eastward from the field of battle, hotly pursued by the Scots, who slew the Danish general, whose name was Mulloch, on the summit of the hill which has since borne his name. The Danes, however, rallied on the hill of Mortlach, behind Aboyne

Castle, where a most sanguinary conflict took place near a stream, thence called the Bleedy Burn; but where fortune still favoured the Scots, and few of their enemies ever returned to their native country to tell the tale of the disastrous campaign.

This is a fair sample of the kind of story current regarding Malcolm Canmore; others of the same popular and quite unhistorical character will be found in Grant's *Legends of the Braes o' Mar*. They do great credit to the inventive faculty of the sennachies of old, but they carry their own refutation in themselves. If history repeats itself, so certainly does invented legend. The twelve Argyllshire men play the part of the gillies at Bannockburn, and the rest of the battle is a rough reproduction of Buchanan's account of the battle of Mortlach in Banffshire, during the reign of Malcolm II., from which the idea of the Danes as foes for Canmore to fight with was probably obtained. It would indeed not be difficult to point to the originals or parallels of most of the legendary tales concerning Canmore. But, as I have said, there is a residuum left after all deductions, and there seems no reason to doubt that the starting-point of all the stories is to be found in the fact that the Scottish King was actually a frequent visitor to the district, and lived in the castle on the island.

As a flash of lightning in a dark night enables the belated wanderer to behold for an instant the position he occupies, so in the midst of the uncertainties of these researches, an actual date cut upon a beam, brought up from the ruins of the old drawbridge, about the year 1782, reveals to us this ancient fortress for a moment in these far-off days. Such at least would seem to be the case if the writer of the Old Statistical Account of the parish of Tullich may be trusted. He says: "The people in the neighbourhood, some years since, were in use to drag up large planks of oak from the bottom of that part of the lake between the island and the mainland on the north side, evidently part of a drawbridge which connected the island with the land; the wood was perfectly fresh and wholesome, and upon one of the planks there was this date, 1113, which is now in the possession of a gentleman in this neighbourhood." This was William Farquharson, of Monaltrie. Unfortunately the plank was afterwards lost sight of, so that the authenticity of the alleged date cannot be tested.

To make clear to the reader the circumstances out of which arose the next event in which the Castle of Kinnord figures, it will be necessary to sketch, however briefly, some portion of the national history following closely on the period at which we have now arrived.

John Strathbogie, Lord of that Ilk, had married Adda, daughter and sole heiress of Henry Hastings, Earl of Atholl, in whose right, on her father's death, he became eighth Earl of Atholl. Taking part with Wallace, he was made prisoner by the English, and put to death with horrible cruelty. His son David, ninth Earl of Atholl and Lord of Strathbogie, wavered in his allegiance between Bruce and Edward; but at last marrying Joan Comyn, daughter and co-heiress of the Red Comyn, whom Bruce had slain at Dumfries, he went over altogether to the English cause. In consequence of this he was disinherited by King Robert, and his lordship of Strathbogie was bestowed upon his former friend, Sir Adam Gordon. David Strathbogie, who had immense estates in England as well as Scotland, made no serious effort to recover the latter, and died in England, leaving a son of his own name, a bold, fickle, and inordinately ambitious young man.

He and some other Scottish exiles had influence enough with the English king to obtain from him a fleet and army with which they invaded Scotland, with the design of regaining by force their forfeited estates and honours, and of dispossessing the present owners. The great Bruce was now dead, and they proposed expelling his son, as yet a young boy, from the throne, and setting up in his room David Balliol, the son of a former king. They thought that if they could do this they would not only repossess themselves of their forfeited properties, but be secured in the possession of them in all time coming. They were very nearly successful; and for two or three years they kept the country in a state of civil war.

David Strathbogie had, through his mother Joan Comyn, inherited the greater part of the fortunes and territorial influence of her once powerful family, and thinking that the former vassals of her house would more readily join his standard if he came among them as the representative of their former lords, he dropped the surname of Strathbogie, and assuming, when in Scotland, that of his mother, called himself David Comyn, though his real name, that which he always took when in England, was David Strathbogie.

Perceiving after a short time that the Scots would never have Balliol for their king, Comyn, as we shall call him, suddenly changed sides in the contest and made his peace with the followers of Bruce, receiving back the earldom of Atholl with the lands belonging to it, and many others besides. He appears to have adopted this line of conduct in pursuance of a deep-laid plan to make himself King of Scotland; and, indeed, if the family of Bruce could have been dispossessed and the family of Balliol rejected, he had the next best claim to the crown. He won over a great many of the Scottish nobility, rode through the country with a train almost royal, appointing his own friends to the command of the castles and forts within his wide domains, but all the while pretending that he was doing so in the interests of King David Bruce. The Castle or Peel of Kinnord he gave to one of his most staunch supporters, Sir Robert Menzies, who had considerable estates in Atholl, and also at Pitfodels, near Aberdeen. He was careful to keep on good terms with the Regent, the brave and loyal Sir Andrew Moray, though there was no man in Scotland he in his heart hated or dreaded more.

When he thought his plans ripe for execution, he threw off his disguise, mustered his followers in Atholl, numbering 3000 foot with some horse, and seizing the opportunity when the Regent was engaged on some business on the eastern border, he hastily marched northward with this force to capture the Castle of Kildrummy, where the Regent's wife, a sister of the late King Robert Bruce, and other royal and noble ladies were then residing. The garrison was brave, but few in numbers; and it is almost a wonder that it was able to resist Atholl's unexpected attack. If it had surrendered, he would have got into his hands almost every member of the Royal Family then resident within the kingdom; for the young king was in France, and the youthful Stewart, the heir apparent, he had already secured.

Christian Bruce, however, found means to despatch a messenger to her husband, who, as has been said, was on the Borders, to inform him of the danger that threatened his family. We may fancy with what consternation and anger the brave Sir Andrew received the intelligence of Atholl's perfidy. But there was not a moment to be lost in unavailing grief and indignation. Hastily collecting 800 brave Border horsemen, among whom was Sir Alexander Gordon, the son and successor of Sir Adam, to whom Bruce had given Atholl's patrimony of Strathbogie, he hurried northward with all possible speed. Comyn, hearing of his approach and fearing a surprise, raised the siege of the Castle, intending either to give the Regent battle at a distance from Kildrummy, where he could not receive succour from the garrison, or where, if he found it necessary, he might make good his retreat into Atholl.

The subsequent events cannot be better told than by paraphrasing, for the sake of the modern reader, the narrative of the ancient chronicler, Wyntoun, whose account is so exact and minute that he must have had his information from an eye-witness.

When Sir Andrew Moray heard how rudely Earl Davy (Atholl) and his men conducted themselves, he was very angry, and prepared to raise the siege forthwith. He therefore collected all the armed men he could obtain to the south of the Scottish Sea (Firth of Forth). The Earl Patrick (Dunbar) joined him, and with him came Ramsay and Preston, and other gentlemen of great renown. William Douglass was also there with his good men and worthy, besides other gentlemen, making in all 800 fighting men; for the flower of that portion of Scotland were then at his

Court. So quick were their movements that they passed the Mounth without stopping.

The Earl Davy (Atholl) now received full information of their approach, and so took his departure from the Castle of Kildrummy. He made straight for Culblean, and there lodged his great array, right in the highway at the east end; and right opposite to where they lay, at the Ha' of Logie Ruthven, Sir Andrew had taken up his quarters. That evening there came to him from Kildrummy 300 "wicht" and hardy men, and this raised the spirits of his own men greatly, and he himself was very glad of their coming.

Well, there was in his army one John of the Craig (John Craig), who had been taken prisoner by Earl Davy, and who would have to pay his ransom next day. This man said privately to the (Scottish) Lords that, if they would take his advice, he would lead them by a short cut through the wood in which their foes lay, and bring them close up to them behind before they would be aware of their approach; and he fulfilled all that he undertook, for between midnight and daybreak he led them where they found the short cut which they followed for more than a mile. Skirting the wood there were two paths; the Earl Davy lay in the lower of these, while the Scots took the higher way, and then struck across to the other. Here every man left his horse, and marched against the foe on foot. These had no knowledge of their approach till well on in the dawn, when they caught sight of them. And then with all the haste they could they warned Earl Davy.

He immediately caused the trumpet to be sounded to warn his soldiers, who in a very short time assembled round him in a small path that was there. Right in the centre of this path stood Earl Davy, and to a great stone that stood beside it,

> "He said, 'Be Goddis face we twa
> The flicht on us sall samen ta'."

which might be paraphrased,

> By thee I stand, and take my oath
> The flight together we take both.

or in the words of Scott,

> "Come one, come all, this rock shall fly
> From its firm base as soon as I."

William Douglass, who then led the vanguard with the stoutest men that were in the company, when he saw Earl Davy stand so arrayed with his men, took his spear in both hands, and, holding it across, said - "Stay, my Lords, a moment." They that were in his company secretly grumbled at this.

When Earl Davy saw that they hesitated, he stepped forward, and cried - "They are already nearly discomfited; upon them with might and main."

After this they withdrew a little bit to a ford, which when Douglass saw, he cried - "Now is our time."

Soon after, they couched their spears and charged in the ford. Robert Brady, a hardy knight, was there slain. A hand-to-hand encounter then took place; and just at that moment Sir Andrew Moray with his company came in stoutly on the flank - so stoutly that they say the bushes bent before them. The moment he appeared the enemy fled; not a single soldier remained to combat.

There by an oak was Earl Davy slain, and several of his followers; Sir William Comyn was also slain; and Sir

Thomas Brown was taken prisoner, and afterwards heavily ironed; for it seems they bore him no good will. Sir Robert Menzies fled to his Castle of Kinnord -

"Thiddyr he went, and in a peil
He sauffit hym and his menye weil."

After a day's reflection, however, he thought better of it, and surrendered and came into his allegiance.

The combatants suffered but little in the fight, we are told, for the defeated side fled "sa hastely, That away gat the mast party." Wyntoun gives us to understand that the battle had been the subject of prophecy by the famous Thomas the Rhymer, but he appears to be sceptical himself as to the alleged power of vaticination.

"This feycht on Sancte Androwis day,
Or on the ewyn, as thai say,
As I dewise, here strekyn was.
Off this feycht qwhilum spak Thomas
Off Erssiltone, that said in derne,*
Thar sulde met stalwart, [stark], and sterne.
He said it in his prophecy,
But how he wist it, was ferly." †

"Thus perished," says a historian, "in the 28th year of his age, David de Strathbogie, of royal descent, nobly allied, and possessing estates above the rank of a subject. He died, seized of the manors of Gainsborough in Lincolnshire, Bullindon in Buckinghamshire, Posewyke, West Lexham, Styvely, and Holkham in Norfolk, Mitford Castle, and other lands in Northumberland. He married Catherine, daughter of Henry Beaumont, styled Earl of Buchan; she survived him and was blockaded in the Castle

*Darkly, obscurely. †A marvel.

of Lochindorb, by Sir Andrew Moray, from November 1335 (immediately after the battle of Culblean), to August 1336, when the siege was raised by Edward III of England."

Another version of the battle of Culblean represents that David Comyn, or Strathbogie, fell by the hand of Sir Alexander Gordon, who had a heavy account of injury to revenge; and that when Sir Robert Menzies escaped to the peel of Loch Kinnord, he was pursued thither by Sir Alexander, and besieged in the island fortress. Sir Robert having previously taken care to have all the boats on the lake secured, in order that if he were obliged to seek safety in the island, his pursuers might not have the means of assaulting the castle, Sir Alexander Gordon quickly set his men to cut down timber and construct rafts, on which they transported themselves to the island, stormed the castle, and put the whole garrison to the sword.

This may be an exaggerated account of what took place; but there is probably some truth in it, though Wyntoun's narrative is the only one to which entire historical credibility must be accorded. Where the other is supplementary, it also may be true; but where contradictory, it must be rejected; and it is certain that Sir Robert Menzies was not put to death, whatever was the fate of his followers.

The consequences of the battle of Culblean were of the most important kind. David, Earl of Atholl, was supposed to be more than a match for the whole Scottish party. In close alliance with the English king, who aided and abetted him in his attempt to secure the crown of Scotland, he seemed to want but the victory at Culblean to secure his object. His slaughter there quenched for ever the hopes of his followers, and did more to strengthen the cause of David Bruce than any other action in the long and disastrous war that arose on the death of the great Bruce. Had David Comyn been successful, and Sir Andrew Moray defeated and slain, the House of Stuart would never have ascended the throne; for Comyn had already made sure of the submission of the young Stuart, the heir apparent of the line of Bruce; and we should have had a Royal House of Comyn, or Strathbogie, with such destiny as Providence might have allotted to it. The battle of Culblean turned the apparently unequal contest, and gave us the fortunes which history records.

What befell the peel or Castle of Loch Kinnord subsequent to the battle of Culblean can only be conjectured. It is about 150 years before its name again appears in any written document that has survived to our day. There is reason, however, to believe that the fort was neither demolished nor disused; and the silence of the chroniclers regarding it may in great part be accounted for by the fact that for the rest of the 14th century the scene of the events which almost exclusively claimed their attention was laid on the distant Borders.

CHAPTER VI

HISTORIC PERIOD

TO 1630 A.D.

WHILE then the national history is occupied in recording a desultory warfare with the English, let us take a glance at the proprietary history of the district in which Loch Kinnord is situated; for it is presumable, though not certain, that the lords of the manor were also the captains of the chief stronghold.

The earliest proprietors of whom we have any certain knowledge were the Bysets, or Bissets, barons of Aboyne. How long they had enjoyed possession of these lands before their name appears in the old charters cannot now be known. They were of Norman descent, and came into Scotland in the reign of William the Lion. By the year 1242 they had become a very powerful family in Scotland, and the chieftainship seemed to rest in Walter Bisset, Lord of Aboyne. For some time a feud had existed between him and Patrick Galloway, Earl of Atholl, who met his death by being burnt in his lodgings in Haddington. Although Walter Bisset proved that at the time of the fire he was entertaining the Queen, Joanna, at his Castle of Aboyne, where she had honoured him with a visit, and whom he had escorted as far as Forfar on her way south, he did not escape the suspicion of having instigated his followers to set fire to the lodgings of Atholl. The end of it was that he was obliged to take refuge in England, where the Queen's brother, Henry III, protected him from his enemies in Scotland.

Although they were declared "forfeit," the lands of Aboyne did not pass out of the hands of his family. The charter-chest of Aboyne is believed to have been rifled by Edward I in 1296, and its contents carried off to England. We can understand why Edward was so anxious to secure these charters. Bisset, in order to be avenged on his Scottish foes, among whom he even included the King, had represented to the English sovereign that the crown of Scotland was a fief of that of England, and that there was evidence of this in the ancient charters. This was just the point that Edward was anxious to establish; and Bisset's own charters were likely to afford the evidence required.

Another Walter Bisset had a charter from King Robert Bruce of the lands of "Aboyne, in the county of Aberdeen." We do not know whether this was a son of old Walter, the exile, or not; but the Bissets had good family reasons for taking the side of Bruce against the Galloways, who were the kinsfolk and abettors of the Balliols.

At this time there were a great many small lairds on Deeside, as elsewhere in Scotland. These held their lands on charters from greater lairds, or Barons; and these, again, from still greater; while the greatest of all, or Lord Superior of the district, held directly of the Crown. Of this last class were the Bissets of Aboyne. In time of war they could have called out the whole military force of the parishes of Glenmuick, Tullich, Glentanar, Aboyne, Birse, and the greater part of Strachan and Durris.

The last of this powerful family, who seems to have

been a son of the last-named Walter Bisset, was Thomas Bisset, to whom David II granted a charter confirming to him the grants made to his ancestors of the lands of Aboyne. The line then terminated in an heiress, who married John Fraser, son of Sir Alexander Fraser and Mary Bruce, second sister of the great King Robert. This marriage, which took place soon after the battle of Culblean, brought the whole lordship of Aboyne into the house of Fraser, to remain there only for one generation.

The eldest daughter of John Fraser, the Lady Margaret Fraser, married Sir William Keith, the great Marischal of Scotland, who received with her the "arrearage and annuels of Aboyne, with other large estates, particularly the Forest of Cowie, the thanedom of Durris, the baronies of Strauchan, Culperso, Johnstone, and many others in the counties of Aberdeen and Kincardine" - a princely "tocher," but then Lady Margaret had royal blood in her veins, and the house of Marischal was second to none in Scotland.

According to the *Records of Aboyne*, Sir William Keith and Margaret Fraser, his wife, held the lands of Aboyne till 1407, when they granted them to their grandson John, Earl of Buchan. On his death the lands reverted to Elizabeth Keith, his aunt, widow of Sir Adam Gordon, and on her death they passed to her daughter Elizabeth, wife of Sir Alex. de Seton, first Lord Gordon, whose descendants were the Earls and Marquises of Huntly and Earls of Aboyne.

It was in the second half of the 15th century that the then Earl of Huntly transferred the principal seat of the family from Gordon in Berwickshire to Strathbogie in Aberdeenshire, but it was many years before the family

Pl. IV.

THE FORMASTON (ABOYNE) STONE

ceased to reside occasionally on their Border estates. Soon after taking up his residence at the Castle of Strathbogie, the Earl directed his attention to the improvement of his Deeside estates, which, having been long in the hands of non-resident owners, had fallen into considerable decay. The fortalice of Aboyne in especial had become uninhabitable, and the fortress of Loch Kinnord, though less decayed, stood much in need of repairs. The latter he rebuilt, not so much as a stronghold as a hunting-seat; and here he generally took up his residence when he visited Deeside. In this condition, serving the purposes of pleasure and the chase, the Castle of Loch Kinnord remained for the rest of the 15th century.

The family papers show that several important transactions took place here during this period. Some vassals attended the Earl to receive renewal of their feudal charters. Among others, Lauchlan Mackintosh, of Galowye, chief of the clan, sought an interview with his lordship at "Lochtcanmor," in the summer of 1497, to grant his bond of manrent, and take the oath of feudal vassalage.

Seven years after this, in the lifetime of Alexander, third Earl of Huntly, the Castle of Loch Kinnord was destined to receive a royal visit under peculiar and rather romantic circumstances. James IV, one of the bravest and best beloved of the kings of the Stuart dynasty, was the soul of chivalry - a disposition which sometimes led him into rather quixotic adventures, and at last proved his ruin. On one occasion, in the year 1505, some conversation having arisen between the King and his courtiers regarding his frequent visits to the shrine of Saint Duthoc in Tain, James undertook, whether as a bet or not is not quite evident, to accomplish the journey, attended only by a chamberlain and squire, for what seemed to them an incredibly small sum of money. It is strange that this freak should have furnished us with one of the clearest glimpses we have of Scottish life and manners at that period; but so it is. Strict accounts had to be kept of every item of expenditure, that it might be seen whether the King had really accomplished what he had undertaken; and these accounts have been preserved. Oh his journey north he lodged in the Castle of Kinnord. There are the following entries in the Accounts of the Lord High Treasurer relating to this visit. "The v day of October, to Jacob Edmanstoun for tursing of the kingis doggis to Loch Canmore, xiiij s." (tursing = setting in order). "Item, the ix day of November [*read* October], to the botmen of Loch Canmor, be the Kingis command, xiiij s. Item, to ane man that provit the watir of Don befor the King, ix s. (October 10th) payit to Schir Peter Crechtoun he gaif, be the Kingis command, to ane blind man in Loch Canmor, v s." We thus see that the King did not scrimp either his munificence or his charity on the occasion of his visiting this quarter.

About the time of this visit, the Earl of Huntly resigned his lands into the hands of the King, and had a re-grant of them, Aboyne, Glenmuick, and Glentanner being included therein, to be named the Barony and Earldom of Huntly "in all future time." The charter is dated 12th January, 1505(6).

In the year 1519, one of the vassals of Earl Alexander appeared at the "pier of Lochtcanmor" to have presence of his lordship, and ask him for a renewal of his lands of Kincraigie, which it would seem the Earl, on account of some offence he had received, was not disposed to grant, and very haughtily refused him an audience. Thereupon the vassal took legal advice, and procuring the services of a notary public, repaired to the end of the drawbridge, and there read his petition and claim. After some time Kincraigie came under the required bondage, and received a renewal of his leasehold.

The Earl of Huntly having married, in his old age, Lady Elizabeth Gray, the widow of Lord Glammis, a designing woman, she took care to secure for herself an ample jointure in case she should survive her lord. This jointure consisted of the Deeside estates, whereof she received a charter from her husband, dated 27th July, 1511, confirmed afterwards by Royal charter - 19th July, 1515. She did survive him, but having no relish for the state of widowhood, she again found connubial bliss with the Earl of Rothes, on whose youth she practised with success the same arts as she had employed on the age of Huntly. Loch Kinnord, with its castle, thus passed in life-rent to an avaricious and non-resident proprietrix, who cared for nothing but the rents. At her death these lands reverted to George, fourth Earl of Huntly, "the proudest, most powerful, and most ambitious of his race." In the early part of his career he was altogether too great a potentate to look after the improvement of this outlying portion of his vast property. He lived at Court and controlled the affairs of the nation till the rising power of the Regent Moray, the head of the reforming party, compelled him to retire to the north.

Here he set himself to repair all the old and decayed fortresses and to build others, with the intention, as his enemies said, of setting up a Highland Principality to overawe the Government. Among others, the Castle of Loch Kinnord was restored to more than its former strength, and garrisoned with a body of the Earl's soldiers. For their spiritual welfare a chapel was built on the southern shore, near the place where the farmhouse of Mickle Kinnord now stands, and where the baptismal font may still be seen. In the chapel they worshipped, and in the consecrated ground around they buried their dead. Although the greater part of the site has now been converted into arable land, the older natives still remember the ruined walls and the green mounds.

It was a stirring time then at Loch Kinnord. Though we have no direct proof, this was in all probability the age when the great drawbridge and the prison on the smaller island were built, and the castle on the larger, and other decayed buildings renovated and made fit for the reception of military. All this came to a sudden end when the plot - whatever it was - was nearly ripe for execution. The great Earl, as is well known, fell in the battle of Corrichie, in 1562; and an indictment of high treason was exhibited against him, his estates and honours being therein declared forfeited to the Crown. This decree did not much trouble his son and successor, who inherited not a little of his father's talents and ambition, because it depended on the issue of the struggle in which he was engaged, as a leader of the party called *Queen's Men*, whether it should have any effect at all. During the time he held the earldom (1562-76), the fort of Loch Kinnord falls quite out of view. It probably still maintained a small garrison to keep Highland cattle-lifters somewhat in check.

George, sixth Earl and first Marquis of Huntly, having

succeeded to the estates and honours of the Earldom when a minor, the management of the property and the leadership of the clan devolved on his uncle, Sir Adam Gordon - the terror of his enemies, and the hero of many a ballad as the famous "Edom o' Gordon." It is not likely that under his regency any strength of the family would have been allowed to fall into decay. We may therefore be very sure that the "Pele" of Loch Kinnord was handed over at his death (1580) to his nephew in as defensible a condition as it had been for the previous century.

The youthful Earl who now succeeded, deprived of the wise counsels of his experienced uncle, displayed at first not a little rashness, extravagance, and pride. He even negotiated with foreign Governments, as if he were an independent sovereign, and affected to despise the Government of his own country. This bearing and action led to the battle of Glenlivet (3rd October, 1594), the result of which was to convince him that, though he had signally defeated a far superior force under Argyll, sent against him by the Government, he had placed himself by his victory in a position of most imminent danger - in fact an untenable position. He therefore submitted to a voluntary exile until the animosity raised against him should subside. On his return to his native land, two years thereafter (13th August, 1596), he was received by the King with great honour, and on 17th April, 1599, created by letters patent first Marquis of Huntly. Whether this favour and these honours had slightly turned his head, or roused the jealousy of the Parliament, certain it is that he very soon after fell under the suspicion of engaging again in treasonable practices against the Government; and from this date till 1616 he was subjected to various periods of imprisonment, and frequently to sentences of excommunication by the Church authorities.

All this persecution - if so we may call it - he bore with a spirit very unlike that which he had displayed in his early youth - a spirit which shows that he was ripening into a great and good man, however mistaken his opinions in politics or his creed in religion may have been. He now eschewed politics and devoted himself with the utmost intelligence to the improvement of his property. He was the first man in the north of Scotland who discovered the advantage of covering its barren moors with plantations of thriving timber, and he led the way for more peaceful times by building mansions, not so much for warlike purposes as for the comforts and conveniences of a more civilized life. In pursuance of this policy, instead of taking up his residence in the fortified "Pele" of Loch Kinnord, he built a new family residence at Kandychyle, on the other side of the Dee, combining, as was still necessary, the means of defence with the conveniences of more peaceful avocations. From this time Kandychyle (Gaelic, *ceann na coille,* "wood-end"), now called Dee Castle, became the principal residence of the Marquis and his family when they visited their Deeside estates.

The chapel, as a matter of course, followed the Marquis's residence and while the one at Loch Kinnord gradually fell into decay, its successor continued, with occasional interruptions and varying fortunes, to hold some ground from 1616 to 1873, when a new Roman Catholic chapel was built at Aboyne, rendering a place of worship at Kandychyle unnecessary, and it has not since been used for that purpose.

The Marquis, we have reason to believe, resided very frequently at Kandychyle. When Spalding, the local historian of the time, has occasion to notice a visit of his lordship, he does so as if it were a thing of common occurrence - for example in July, 1633, "the Marquess of Huntlie, intending to keip his Parliament, cam to Kandechyle, quhair he thair fell sek"; and again next year he takes journey from the north to Edinburgh, but fell sick at Kandychyle.

It would seem also, from the traditions that still circulate in the district regarding the place, that it was used mainly, if not entirely, as a hunting-seat, and that it was seldom occupied for military purposes. "On the hill of Little Tullich," says the writer of the New Stat. Account, "overlooking the site of the old Castle of *Ceann-na-coille* are the remains of what is called 'My Lord's House,' consisting of five courses of a square stone building, the wall at the base course 12 feet thick, and diminishing about a foot each course, so that the five courses present, on the outside, the appearance of a stair of so many steps on each side. The entry is from the west, and the apartment within is 7 1/2 feet each side. The use of this building is reported to have been for obtaining a view during a deer-hunt."

It may be allowable so far to digress from the direct narrative as to say that the skilled workmen employed in the building of the new castle at *Ceann na coille* were brought by the Marquis from the town of Huntly. After the completion of the work several of these settled on the Deeside estates, and afterwards became industrious and respected tenants. The Robertsons, the Milnes, and the

Calders trace their origin as tenants on Deeside to the above circumstance. Their forebears were artificers in stone, iron, and timber, and settled ultimately in Balletrach, Glentanar, and Greystone of Inchmarnoch.

It was in the family of the first-named that the youthful Lord Byron resided for some time, when recovering from an attack of fever; and the name of one member has been immortalized by obtaining a place in his poetry. Mary Robertson, the second daughter, had won the boyish affection of the young poet; and though he might say,

"It could not be love, for I knew not the name,"

certain it is that her image was not effaced from his memory even in the later years of his life. Mary was not generally esteemed such a beauty as her elder sister, Jean; but the writer has it from one that knew her in her bloom, that "she was a bonnie lassie for a' that." It may interest the reader to know something of the after life of "Byron's Mary," as (after the publication of his "Hours of Idleness") she was generally called in the district. Her parents were not wealthy, but her mother was well connected. Helen Bland Watson Macdonald, afterwards Mrs. Robertson of Balletrach, was the daughter of Captain Macdonald of Rinetan, whose descent can, it is said, be traced from a Lord of the Isles. Mr. Robertson had a large family; one of the younger sons, named Lewis, was playfully styled "Lewis XIII," to mark his place among the other members; and hence arose a saying that one of the kings of France was born at Balletrach. Through Captain Macdonald's influence three of the sons obtained commissions in the service of the H.E.I.C., and all rose to the rank of Colonel. Other two members of the family were educated for the Roman Catholic priesthood, but, it is believed, they never entered into orders, owing it is said to some difficulties in regard to their taking the oath of celibacy. Mary, Lord Byron's first flame, married Kenneth Stewart, an Excise officer, then stationed in the parish of Crathie. At his death, which occurred very soon after their marriage, she removed to Aberdeen, where she died; but her remains were conveyed to the old churchyard of Glentanar, where there is a handsome tombstone over her grave, bearing the following inscription:-

> "Sacred to the memory of James Robertson, who departed this life on 4th day of April, 1814, aged 71 years; and of Helen Macdonald, his spouse, who died on 11th day of August, 1813, aged 60 years; Also of MARY ROBERTSON, their daughter, widow of Kenneth Stewart, who died at Aberdeen on 2nd March, 1867, aged 85 years."

It thus appears that Mary Robertson - "My Sweet Mary" - was the poet's senior by six years.

Even at that early age (nine and ten) the wilful, intractable disposition, which in riper years too much distinguished the character of the noble bard, had begun to display itself. The following is the account the author received, from the late Mrs. Stephen, who lived at Greystone, the farm adjoining Balletrach. She was a little girl of six or seven at the time of Byron's residence on Deeside, and remembered him well. "He was a very takan' laddie," she used to say, "but nae easily managed. He was very fond of coming up to see my father's shop [a carpenter's workshop], and particularly fond o' the turning-lathe; but he widna haud his hands fae ony o' the tools, and he spoiled them completely before he would let them go. My father couldna lay hands on him, and he wid tak' nae tellan' ; so at last he always set some o' us to watch when we wid see him coman' up the brae fae Balletrach; and when he got word that he was coman' he would lock the door an' gang awa' out about. There was nae ither way o' deean' wi' him."

CHAPTER VII

CIVIL WAR

TO 1645 A.D.

THE Aboyne peerage, with the holders of which the Castle of Loch Kinnord and surrounding lands are henceforth mainly associated, took its rise in 1627, when King Charles I, by letters patent, created Lord John Gordon, second son of the first Marquis of Huntly, Viscount of Melgum and Lord Aboyne. But the young lord did not long enjoy his new title, having been burnt to death in the house of Frendraught, in October, 1630; and with his death the peerage became extinct.

Two years after a new peerage was created by patent, dated at Whitehall, 20th April, 1632, reciting that "We being informed of the lamentable death of the late Viscount of Melgum, and well knowing the good service performed to us by his elder brother, George, Lord Gordon, and being willing that the former title of Viscount should be revived in the family," etc. The patent then proceeds in due form to create George, Lord Gordon, eldest son of the (first) Marquis of Huntly, Viscount of Aboyne, during the life of his father, with a limiting clause to the effect that, should he survive his father and succeed to the Marquisate, the title of Viscount of Aboyne should then descend to his *second* son, James, and his heirs male bearing the name of Gordon. On the decease of his father, the first Marquis of Huntly, in

1636, he did succeed to the estates and honours, and the Aboyne peerage descended in terms of the patent to his second son, James, who now became second Viscount of Aboyne. He may be said to have been a man of war from his youth, for scarcely had he succeeded to the peerage when he had to draw the sword, as leader of the clan in defence of the King against the Covenanters. His father and elder brother being then prisoners in Edinburgh, he mustered their vassals for the purpose of repelling an invasion of their lands by the Earl of Montrose. A battle took place at Bridge of Dee near Aberdeen, 19th June, 1639, in which Aboyne was defeated, and whence he soon afterwards escaped by sea into England: "To Bervick [to the King] gois he."

A lull now occurred in the military operations of both parties, during which the Marquis and Lord Gordon were liberated from their imprisonment in Edinburgh Castle, but it was only the calm before the storm. The House of Huntly was at this time unusually strong in military talent, but it had also unusual difficulties to contend with. The clan was by far the most powerful in the north, but then the whole military strength of the south and west was arrayed against it; and though the chief and his four eldest sons were able commanders, they were seldom all agreed in counsel, and often acted in opposition to each other. With such sources of internal weakness in the presence of watchful and powerful enemies, the house of Gordon could not stand; and so it proved.

Hostilities were renewed in the north by the Marquis of Argyll, who, under pretence of putting down some Highland marauders, invaded the lands of Lochaber and

Badenoch. "This done, he disbandis his army, and cumis doun Diesyde, about 1200 men. Bot what ordour he tuke with the brokkin men, oppressouris of the countrie, wes not mekill hard, so forduard wes he for the Covenant." This was the first visit Deeside had the honour of receiving from the Argyllshire men during these troubles, and it occurred in the month of June or July, 1640. There was little damage done to the Gordon lands by this invasion. The two great lords, Huntly and Argyll, were as yet on good terms, and brothers-in-law, Huntly having married Argyll's eldest sister, so there was no "spuilzie" committed this time.

Next year, 1641, a great calamity befell the Huntly property on Deeside. The fine mansion which the late Marquis had built at Kandychyle (Dee Castle) for his summer residence in these parts had been let to a military officer of the name of Garden, who had been stationed here with some soldiers to take order with the "broken" men. Whether it was through the negligence of Garden, or, as some with better reason suppose, by the hands of these broken men, who naturally desired to be quit of his presence, certain it is that "upon the 23rd of Marche, the place of Kandichyll, pertening to the Lord Marques, by ane suddant fyre; is rakleslie brynt and distroyit, his haill insicht and plenishing consumeit, to his gryte skaith." Huntly was not disposed quietly to submit to this great loss, in whatever way the fire might have originated; and Crowner Garden was compelled to agree and pay the Marquis for the damage his mansion had sustained. Kandychyle was not again rebuilt till after the troublous times of the Civil War were ended, soon after which it again appears, though only as a shooting-lodge, the old castle having become a ruin.

Three years later, namely in 1644, the two great parties, Covenanters and anti-Covenanters, having become irreconcilable enemies to each other, both prepared to draw the sword in terrible earnest. Huntly, holding the Royal Commission of Lieutenancy of the north, assumed the command of the latter and set vigorously about marshalling his vassals and clan for the coming struggle. For this purpose he came to Deeside and fixed his headquarters at Aboyne. We may form some idea of the power of the Gordons at this time when we learn that their chief, at the great gathering of the clan on this occasion, "came from Aboyne, where he had many Highlandmen and footmen there, and in the country about, attending his service. He came to Aberdeen with about two hundred horse and eight hundred foot, which were reckoned in the Links when they were drilled." Spalding, the contemporary historian, adds that "he had few commanders besides himself, Crowner King, and Major Nathaniel Gordon." If the reader should ask where were his brave sons, we have to answer that his eldest son and heir, the Lord Gordon, was with the Covenanters; the second son, James Viscount Aboyne, was with the king in England; the third son, Lewis, had terribly offended his father, who refused to repose any trust in him; and the fourth, Charles, who many years after became first Earl of Aboyne, was a young lad at school in Aberdeen.

On the approach of an army 6,000 strong, led by the Marquis of Argyll, the Earl Marischal, and the Lord Gordon, Huntly disbanded his followers and retired, first to Strathbogie, and afterwards to a lonely isle in Strathnaver,

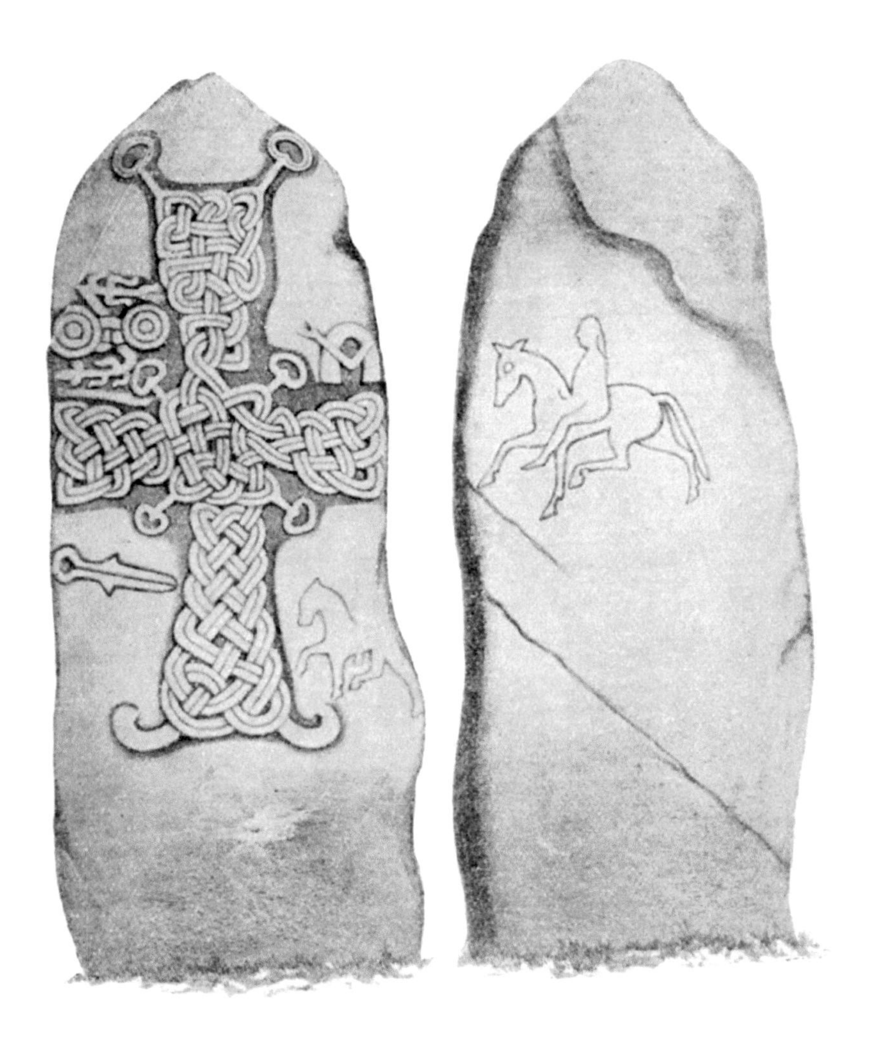

Pl. V.

THE MIGVIE STONE

in the extreme north-west of Sutherlandshire, where he lay concealed for a long time. Meanwhile "cam to Cromar, Brass, Oboyne, Strathauchin and countreis about, 800 Argile Hieland men, quhair they had in allowanss ilk day, to be takin of the countrie, 24 bollis meill, sex scoir wedderis, and - mairtis, with thrie scoir dolleris of money. And thay leivit vpone the Marques of Huntleis landis of Cromar, Glenmvk, and Glentanner . . . . fra thair cuming thair, quhilk wes upon the day of May quhill [till] the third day of Junij," They did not, however, leave on the 3rd of June, but continued to infest and plunder the country for a month longer.

During the next month a split took place among the Covenanters. They had already been diverging into two parties, whom we may call the Moderates and the Radicals. At the head of the former was Montrose, and at the head of the latter, which was the stronger party, was Argyll. The Lord Gordon strongly sympathised with the opinions of Montrose but he was for some time restrained from taking part with him by the influence which his uncle Argyll possessed over him. When the rupture could no longer be avoided, Montrose hastily broke with the party and went over to the King, by whom he was graciously received and appointed his lieutenant in Scotland. Viscount Aboyne, as already stated, was also at Court; and it is likely that he and Montrose concerted the plan of a rising in the Highlands. The Gordons were now without a head, but their fiery spirits could not brook the daily insults and spoilzies to which they were subjected, and no sooner did Montrose set up the Royal Standard than they hastened, though in detached and independent parties, to join him. In consequence of this the Lords of the Covenant issued an order for the demolition of the castles and houses belonging to such of the clan as were suspected or known to be anti-Covenanters. Among these are mentioned Abergeldie, Aboyne, Whitehouse in Cromar, and Auchterfoul (now Wester Coull), "which by the Parliament were ordained to be casten down to the ground"; "yet it pleased God that the houses were not casten down but yet stand still."

Montrose being now at the head of a considerable body of troops marched northward, while the Covenanting, or Parliamentary army, lying at Aberdeen, under command of Argyll, Marischal, and the Lord Gordon, prepared to dispute the passage of the Dee. The wary Montrose, however, gave them the slip, crossed the Dee at Crathes, and marched boldly into the heart of the Gordon lands, taking care that his soldiers should commit no act of spoliation or oppression. Argyll and his company followed at the head of a superior force, but always at a safe distance from the enemy; and in this way the two armies passed through the Garioch, Strathbogie, and Speyside. Here Argyll lost sight of his foe, who next appeared in the Carse of Gowrie, marching to the siege of Dundee.

Meanwhile Argyll's foot army scattered themselves over the land of the anti-Covenanting Gordons and others, "cutting down the pleasant garden plantings to be huts, destroying the corns, and left not a four-footed beast in the lands of Drum, Cromar, Auchterfoul, Aboyne, Abergeldie, and the country about." This was a much heavier loss and oppression to the poor people than the visitation of the *Cleansers* in the months of May and June; for it was now the month of October, and the ingathering of the harvest nearly completed, such a spoilzie and destruction placed them face to face with famine and starvation during the winter.

Before the winter came on however, Montrose, wheeling about from Angus, in a few days swooped down upon these marauders, who fled in all haste, some to Aberdeen, some home to Argyllshire. It was a case of "Chevy Chase." Again the two armies followed each other very nearly as before, and neither appeared again on Deeside till the spring of the following year; before which time Lord Gordon and his third brother, Lord Ludovic or Lewis, had separated themselves from the Covenanters and were serving the King under Montrose, who then lay encamped at Kirriemuir.

"Understanding sum enemeis war risin and growing to ane heid (*i.e.*, collecting their forces) sic as Frendraught, the Frasers, Forbeses, and their kin and freindis and cheifly against the hous of Huntly and their friends and follouers, Montrose most wisely directs from Kirriemuir the Lord Gordon's brother, Lewis, or Lord Lewis, with about a hundred and sixty horsemen, to go home and defend his awin country and friends." By this time, however, the Covenanters in these parts had gathered to a great head, and were holding their committees in Aberdeen for uptaking of the excise and laying additional burdens upon the king's subjects. The Lord Gordon himself was therefore despatched with orders to dissolve the committee. Passing the Mounth, still white with snow, he crossed the Dee at Mill of Dinnet upon the 8th day of April 1645, and directing his course down Deeside, the committee suddenly dispersed like pigeons at the approach of a hawk. Lord Gordon then passed through the country taking order with his enemies; and strengthening his castles, fixed the head-quarters of his army in Morayshire, whither the parliament sent Major Hurry in pursuit of him, while General Baillie was directed to keep his eye upon Montrose, who still kept moving about in Angus and Perthshire, with the view of effecting a junction with the Viscount Aboyne, who with other gentlemen were, he had been informed, on their way from the king to join him if possible. As soon as Aboyne and his company arrived, Montrose gave Baillie the slip, passed the mountains, and crossing the Dee with his whole force at Mill of Crathes, sent Aboyne with a detachment to Aberdeen to procure ammunition, moving himself by way of Skene to effect a junction with the Lord Gordon, now threatened by Major Hurry. All these movements having been successfully executed, Baillie, thus out-generalled, hastened to the succour of Hurry, who by this time was as far north as Morayshire on rather a wild-goose chase, as the Lord Gordon had doubled round and was now united with Montrose. On the 10th of May 1645, Baillie's army, about 2000 foot and 120 troopers, passed the Cairn o' Mounth, and encamped in Birse. Next day, which was Sunday, they marched into Cromar, and encamped on the flat ground betwixt the kirks of Tarland and Coull. Here he resolved to await reinforcements, and sent directions to Hurry so to move his forces that the two Parliamentary armies should approach each other; but in the position of the armies no messenger could reach Hurry, as he would have to pass the enemy's lines, and Montrose was too wise a general to let his enemies communicate with each other, if he could prevent it. Montrose had thus the fullest information regarding their purposes, while Baillie at least was even ignorant where his colleague lay. He therefore kept his camp in Cromar, "plundering and eiting the grein growing cornes scarss cum to the blaid," while Montrose dealt with his colleague Hurry, at Auldearn, where he utterly defeated him in a "bloody battle in which the Lord Gordon and the Viscount of Aboyne, and their name and followers, fought so valiantly that they deserved eternal praise."

As soon as Baillie heard of this defeat "he lifts frae Cromar with all speed, and hastens to Strathbogie," with the view of affording protection to the scattered remnants of Hurry's forces. This was a judicious movement, and gave Montrose no little trouble, because for some weeks after the battle of Auldearn he was almost as weak as the general he had vanquished; "for his Highlanders must needs have time to rin hame wi' the spoilzie."

A series of manoeuvres now took place between the two armies, Montrose evading battle till his Highlanders should return, and Baillie wishing to draw him into action. In the course of these movements Montrose lay for a time encamped in Cromar, in the vicinity of Loch Kinnord, while Baillie approached him from the direction of Aberdeen. Montrose then moved his forces to the old Castle of Corgarff, where he awaited the incoming of his Highlanders. When these had assembled in sufficient numbers he resolved to give his adversary battle, and drawing him into a favourable position for himself near the village of Alford, he attacked and signally defeated him,

(2nd July 1645), the Gordons on this occasion as at Auldearn bearing the brunt of the battle and achieving the victory.

The victory however, brilliant as it was, was dearly bought by the death of the young chief of the Gordons. As I consider the character of the Lord Gordon, who fell in the battle of Alford in the flower of his age, inferior in bravery, generosity, and magnanimity to that of very few of his noble ancestors, I shall not scruple, even in this brief historical sketch, to give at some length the opinion formed of him by competent contemporary writers:- "Lord Gordon was a very hopeful young gentleman, able of mind and body, about the age of 28 years." "There was," says Wishart, "a general lamentation for the loss of the Lord Gordon whose death seemed to eclipse all the glory of the victory. As the report spread among the soldiers, every one appeared to be struck dumb with the melancholy news, and a universal silence prevailed for some time through the army. However, their grief burst through all restraints, venting itself in the voice of lamentation and sorrow. When the first transports were over the soldiers exclaimed against heaven and earth for bereaving the king, the kingdom, and themselves of such an excellent young nobleman; and unmindful of the victory or the plunder, they thronged about the body of their dead captain, some weeping over the wounds and kissing his lifeless limbs, while others praised his comely appearance even in death, and extolled his noble mind, which was enriched with every valuable qualification that could adorn his high birth or ample fortune; they even cursed the victory bought at so dear a rate. Nothing could have supported the army under this immense sorrow but the presence of Montrose, whose safety gave them joy, and not a little revived their drooping spirits. In the meantime he could not command his grief, but mourned bitterly over the melancholy fate of his only and dearest friend, grievously complaining that one who was the honour of his nation, the ornament of the Scots nobility, and the boldest assertor of the Royal authority in the north, had fallen in the flower of his youth."

CHAPTER VIII

CIVIL WAR

TO 1647 A.D.

MONTROSE was doomed very soon to feel the loss he had sustained in the death of Lord Gordon; for the Marquis of Huntly, now living in concealment in Strathnaver, hearing of the death of his eldest son, and of the brilliant career of Montrose, of whose fame he was always jealous, returned to his own country, and the Gordons were never undividedly true to Montrose afterwards. His defeat at Philiphaugh gave Huntly a pretext for acting an independent part, of which he was not slow to take advantage, but though he had the ambition he had not the talent to take the place of Montrose; and his jealousy and family pride ruined both, and ultimately brought both to the scaffold in the same cause.

Trusting to be supported by the Gordons, Montrose proceeded to the north, and, for appearance' sake, was joined by some of the clan headed by the Viscount Aboyne, now the eldest surviving son, and Lord Lewis Gordon, his next brother; but the influence of their father, who never ceased to upbraid them with overlooking the importance of the family and lending their assistance to his rival, in a short time weakened the attachment of the young men to Montrose, whom they soon afterwards deserted with the whole of their followers.

The noble-minded Montrose, however, did not retaliate, but marching from Alford through Cromar, passed Loch Kinnord, pursued his course up Deeside, and crossing the Cairnwell pitched his camp in Strathardle, and there waited for the reinforcements which had been promised him both by Viscount Aboyne, when he took his leave, and by other Highland chieftains. These failing to arrive at the appointed time, and his own army being too weak to carry out any successful invasion of the south, he again directed his course northward, in the hope that if he could obtain a personal interview with Huntly he might be able to induce him to co-operate with him in bringing the country over to the interest of the king. Huntly greatly dreaded a personal interview with Montrose and had taken steps to evade it, but they were rendered ineffectual by the skill and activity of his more experienced fellow-general. Leaving his little army near Kinnord and selecting a small bodyguard of light cavalry, he struck across the country; and one morning while Huntly, believing that the royal army were lying with their general somewhere in Atholl or Braemar, was in fancied security sitting down to breakfast, who should ride up to the door of the Bog of Gight but Montrose with fifty or sixty horsemen? There was no avoiding the interview; and he made the best of the untoward meeting, promising, though in a half-hearted way, co-operation. A plan was arranged between the two for the reduction of the Castle of Inverness. They were to approach it from different points, Montrose from the Highlands, Huntly from the Lowlands of Morayshire. The former, directing his army from Cromar through Strathspey, was soon at his post; but the latter, leaving to his rival the task - hopeless in the circumstances - of reducing the Castle of Inverness, wheeled round and marched towards Aberdeen, which he intended to surprise and capture, and thus emulate his military glory.

When he had proceeded as far as Kintore, he was joined by the Earl of Crawford with Montrose's horse; but hearing that General Middleton was approaching to the relief of Aberdeen with a parliamentary army, he suddenly changed his plan and broke up his forces into two divisions, with the one of which he and Crawford retired to Banff, while the other under Viscount Aboyne marched up Deeside and fixed their head-quarters near Loch Kinnord, the castle and fortifications of which they were employed for the next three months in repairing and strengthening. This work was set about in the end of February, or early in March 1646, and the force employed on it is estimated at not less than a thousand men; but as many of them were Highlanders, who considered manual labour an indignity, the work performed, it may well be supposed, was not commensurate with the hands employed. However that may have been, there is reason to believe that the place was rendered one of considerable strength.

Ever since the removal of the family residence to Kandychyle, the fort of Loch Kinnord had been allowed to fall into decay. This would appear from the fact that, although both royalist and parliamentary generals had during the wars of the Covenant several times passed and repassed the lake, and encamped in its vicinity, it is only but once mentioned by any of the writers who record these events. During that period it would seem therefore to have been of small importance in a military point of view. The

Marquis of Huntly now (spring of 1646) restored it, and garrisoned it with a body of soldiers in name of the king.

When the Marquis found himself relieved of the presence of General Middleton, who about the end of May set out from Aberdeen in pursuit of Montrose, he resolved to carry out his plan of capturing that city, which was now defended only by a small cavalry force under Colonel Montgomery. "Accordingly he ordered his men to march from Deeside to Inverurie, where he appointed a general rendezvous to be held." He succeeded in capturing the town, with a loss on his side of only about twenty men in all. He has been severely blamed for allowing it to be plundered by his soldiery, but there is at least this excuse to offer for him, that although the "brave town" did not deserve it at his hands, it was probably not in his power to restrain the marauding disposition of his wild Highlanders, whose sole motive for being under arms was spoil, and who looked upon the spoil as their rightful reward. Laden with plunder, these Highlanders escaped to their homes to deposit the spoilzie, and Huntly suddenly found himself, with greatly reduced numbers, liable to be cut off by General Middleton, who might very soon be expected from the north. Leaving Aberdeen therefore, he moved back to his old quarters at Loch Kinnord, whither he was very soon followed by Middleton, and, after some skirmishing at the Pass of Ballater, compelled to retire to Braemar; and Middleton, not caring to follow him thither, returned to Aberdeen. This occurred about the middle of June 1646, and before the month had closed the King, who had surrendered to the Scottish army, ordered both Montrose and Huntly to disband their forces. The war for the moment was therefore at an end.

Had the war finally ended here, the lives of both these noblemen might have been saved and their estates in great part secured to them and their descendants; while the fort of Loch Kinnord, crumbling slowly under the weight of years, would still have presented a magnificent ruin. A very different fate awaited it.

Before six months had passed, the King, who was then under a sort of honourable confinement with the Scottish army near Newcastle, perceiving that he would be surrendered to the English Parliament, and in that case dreading the worst, sent a secret message to Huntly to raise his forces, and he would attempt to escape and join him in the north. The Marquis did so, but the plot was discovered and frustrated. This placed him in an exceedingly difficult and dangerous position. He was now a rebel in the eyes of the law, for the King had surrendered his authority to the Scottish Estates, against whom he had again drawn the sword after having come to terms with them. In these straits he continued to keep his forces together, and was even successful in defeating Major Bickerton, who had been sent to capture him.

At the approach, however, of General David Leslie, he disbanded his little army, and with a few staunch followers fled to the mountains of Lochaber for shelter. "Leslie thereupon reduced the castles belonging to the Marquis." He first took that of Strathbogie, in which house was Lord Charles Gordon (afterwards Earl of Aboyne), who, with Newton the governor, was made prisoner; then the neighbouring Castle of Lesmore; then, marching northward, he took Gordon Castle, or Bog of Gight, as it was then called. Marching southward, he "tooke the Isle of Loghtannor [*read* Loghtcannor] in Aboyn, which Huntley hade fortified," and established a garrison there.*

Thereafter General Leslie marched into Badenoch in quest of the Marquis, but not finding him there, he captured the Castle of Ruthven, another strong fortress of the Gordons, and proceeded into Lochaber, where he took in their remaining Highland stronghold, the Castle of Inverlochy; and thence advanced to the subjugation of the Western Isles, leaving the pursuit of his lordship to General Middleton. Huntly succeeded for several months in eluding the hot pursuit of his enemies, living in dens, caves, and the recesses of deep forests in the most inaccessible parts of the Highlands. A reward of £1000 sterling was now offered by the Committee of Estates to any person who should apprehend him - an exploit which was accomplished by Colonel Menzies in the following manner. Middleton was lying with his army in Strathbogie, while his officers with their dragoons were scouring the country far and wide in quest of the fugitive, who but a few years before was almost absolute lord of all that region. In one of these excursions, "Menzies, having received intelligence of the place of the Marquis's retreat, got the command of a select body of horse, consisting of three troops, with which he proposed to surprise and capture his lordship. Huntly's place of concealment was well chosen. It was the

*The accounts which we have of the taking of these strengths in "Gordon's Continuation" are provokingly meagre. Enough is said to show that some of them at least were bravely defended, while not a single detail of interest is given.

farmhouse of Dalnabo, at the junction of the rivers Allanach and Avon, three miles below Inchrory. Close by the house was a deep narrow defile, cut out of the old sandstone rock by the impetuous torrent of the Allanach. In case of danger he might retreat thither, where he would be safe from the pursuit of any species of cavalry, and where a few resolute followers might defend him against almost any number of assailants. Menzies was probably aware of this, and made his arrangements accordingly. It was in the dead of winter, towards the end of December 1647, when the season of the year and the inaccessible nature of the hiding-place produced a feeling of security and a remissness in the watch. About midnight, just as the Marquis was going to bed, the tramp of horsemen was heard at the door." Huntly was attended by only ten gentlemen and servants as a body-guard, who, notwithstanding the great disparity of numbers, made a brave attempt to protect their master, in which six of them were killed and the rest mortally wounded, among whom was John Grant, the landlord. On hearing that the Marquis had been taken prisoner, the whole of his vassals in the neighbourhood, to the number of 400 or 500, with Grant of Carron* at their head, flew to arms to rescue him. Menzies, dreading that a rescue would be attempted, carried the Marquis in all haste to Blairfindie in Glenlivet, where his lordship received secret intimation that his followers had solemnly sworn that they would either rescue him or die to a man. However, he dissuaded them from the intended

*This was the notorious Seumas an tuim (" James of the hillock,") one of the most daring of outlaws, who had long held the post of Captain of broken, or hill men, in these parts.

attempt and sent them word "that, now almost worn out with grief and fatigue, he could no longer live in hills and dens; and hoped that his enemies would not drive things to the worst; and, if such was the will of Heaven, he could not outlive the sad fate he foresaw his royal master was likely to undergo; and, be the event as it would, he doubted not but the just providence of God would restore the royal family, and his along with it."

From Strathbogie the Marquis was carried under a strong guard of horse to Leith, where he was delivered to the magistrates and thrown into jail. The Committee pressed for an immediate execution, and his life was spared till the meeting of Parliament, by a majority of only one vote.

The Marquis languished in prison from December 1647 till March 1649, for during the lifetime of the king the Parliament had not ventured to bring him to the block; but the king himself had during the interval been put to death, and the Parliament, no longer under restraint, on 16th March ordered the Marquis of Huntly to be beheaded on the 22nd of the same month at the Market Cross of Edinburgh. When the fatal day came he ascended the scaffold with a firm step, and turning "to the people, he told them that he was going to die for having employed some years of his life in the service of the king, his master; that he was sorry he was not the first of his Majesty's subjects who had suffered for his cause, so glorious in itself that it sweetened to him all the bitterness of death." He then declared that he had charity to forgive those who had voted for his death, although he could not admit that he had done anything contrary to the laws. He then offered up a prayer, and embracing some friends around him, submitted his neck without any symptom of emotion to the fatal instrument.*

During the time Huntly lay in prison, Argyll bought up all the "comprisings" on his estates, "and caused summon at the Market Cross of Aberdeen, by sound of trumpet, all his wadsetters and creditors to appear at Edinburgh in the month of March following the Marquis's imprisonment, calling on them to produce their securities before the Lords of Session, with certification that if they did not appear their securities were to be declared null and void." Some of these creditors sold their claims to Argyll, and having thus bought up all the rights he could obtain upon Huntly's estate at a small or nominal value, under pretence that he was acting for the benefit of his nephew, the Viscount Aboyne, he granted bonds for the amount, which Spalding says he never paid. In this way did Argyll possess himself of the Marquis's estates, which he continued to enjoy for upwards of twelve years, viz., from 1648 to 1660.

And where was this nephew of whose interests he took such tender care? Although the father was hunted down at Dalnabo, his four surviving sons managed to escape from their pursuers, and fled the country. The two eldest, James Viscount Aboyne and Lord Lewis, went to Paris; Charles, afterwards created Earl of Aboyne, had, as already noticed, been taken prisoner and narrowly escaped the fate of his father, and his youngest brother Henry went abroad and ultimately took service under the King of Poland. When James heard of the execution of Charles I,

*A fine portrait of his Lordship, styled "Marquis of Gordon," is in Pinkerton's "Scottish Gallery."

he sunk into a melancholy and in a few days after died of the grief it gave him; and with him, who died without issue, the Viscounty of Aboyne became extinct.

Argyll's management of the property of his brother-in-law the Marquis of Huntly was of a piece with his tender regard for the life of him and his family. Probably still apprehensive that a counter-revolution might arise which might restore their fortunes, his first object was to see that the fortresses in which their strength had lain should be destroyed. General Leslie, who had captured these in 1647, had no instruction to dismantle them, and he probably did them little injury. In the month of June 1648, just fourteen months after the capture by Leslie and six months after the apprehension of the Marquis at Dalnabo, Argyll procured an Act of Parliament to effect his object, in which "the fortifications of Loch Kender are ordered to be *slighted* ". The *slighting* ordered by the Parliament meant their utter demolition, which was soon after very effectually executed. Time and the utilitarian hands of engineers and others have done the rest, and left this once and long celebrated lake and fortress as it is this day.

CHAPTER IX

ARCHAEOLOGY AND RELICS OF ANTIQUITY

THE antiquarian relics which have been found in, or in the immediate neighbourhood of the loch, so far as they are known to the writer, may be conveniently grouped according to the material of which they are composed.

OBJECTS OF WOOD. - As early as the middle of the 18th century, great numbers of logs of black oak had been recovered from the loch, and speculation then began to be rife regarding the purposes they might have originally served. At that time a large quantity of the timbers of the bridge or gangway connecting the Castle Island with the north shore were still in situ, though they were rapidly disappearing, being considered by the natives as common property, and much valued in the manufacture of agricultural and other implements and ornaments. When the first stone bridge was being erected at Ballater (1780-1) the beams of oak were so numerous and in so sound a condition that they were found sufficient to form the foundations on which the stone piers were built.*

*This bridge was swept away by the great flood of 1799; another handsome stone bridge shared the same fate in 1829, which after some years was replaced by a wooden structure, and that now by an elegant

Pl. VI.

CRANNOG ON LOCH KINNORD

The great drought of the summer of 1826 caused such a scarcity of water in the district that, to supply the Mill of Dinnet with motive power, Loch Kinnord was used as a reservoir, and its surface slightly lowered. This draining of the water brought to light many relics of the ancient buildings and a good deal more of the structure of the bridge, the beams of which, along with much other oak timber found in various parts of the lake, were dragged ashore and shared the same fate as those previously recovered. The brothers William and John MacPherson, Bogangore, long preserved an oaken beam as a specimen of this material. Though by no means one of the largest, it measured 24 feet long and 14 inches on the side of the square.

Some years subsequent to 1826 a boat was discovered in the mud at the bottom of the loch, and dragged ashore by the people in the neighbourhood. It was substantially built of oak planks, the overlap being stuffed with tarred wadding and secured with iron bolts well made and skilfully rivetted. It probably belonged to the last era of the Castle, or the first half of the 17th century, and might have been sunk at the time it was dismantled. Everything recovered from the loch was about this time considered to have belonged to Malcolm Canmore, and a boat of that age became such an object of curiosity to both natives and visitors that having no protection it became a prey to vandal hands and speedily disappeared. The exact dimensions cannot now be ascertained, but William MacPherson, who had examined it, informed

and substantial granite bridge, which it is to be hoped will have a longer reign than any of its predecessors.

the writer, with his characteristic admiration of everything ancient, that it was coble-shaped, and in point of workmanship would compare favourably "wi' the best boats they can mak' noo-a-days, for a' they think o' themsels." Broken planks of boats have frequently been found buried in the mud, several of them so rudely shaped as to indicate that they belonged to an age long anterior to the 17th century.

In the summer of 1858 a second lowering of the level took place, the combined effect of the two being a reduction of about 3 feet. Various relics of antiquity were discovered in different parts of the loch at this time. Among others a canoe, which had been observed sometime previously near the north shore and opposite the smaller island, was by the lowering of the water level brought so near the surface that it appeared practicable to drag it ashore. Accordingly next year, leave having been obtained from the Marquis of Huntly, about fifty persons belonging to the neighbourhood assembled, and by means of ropes and long poles succeeded in raising and bringing to land the Royal Yacht, for such it was immediately christened. It was of large dimensions and in a wonderful state of preservation considering the length of time it must have lain so near the surface of the water. In length it measured 22½ feet, and was 3 feet 4 inches wide at the stern. The width here had been somewhat increased by a rent in the bottom owing to which the sides had spread out a little. The thickness of the keel was about 4 inches throughout; and the greatest depth inside about 9 inches, but the edges or gunwales were much worn down, and the depth inside proportionately diminished. The thickness of the stern was 1 foot 6 inches. From the stern the breadth of the canoe gradually decreased till at 6 feet from the prow it measured 2 feet 9 inches; from this point it tapered rapidly to a sharp point. In the bottom there were two very considerable rents - one-5 feet long opened into the stern, the other 7 feet 10 inches long, but not so wide as the other, began at 5 feet from the stern and extended towards the bows. These rents seem to have showed themselves while the canoe was in use; for it had undergone some curious repairs evidently for the purpose of obviating these defects. The repairs consist of two bars of

FIG. 4. - CANOE FOUND IN LOCH KINNORD

oak sunk longitudinally directly under the rents to the depth of about an inch into the keel of the canoe, and fixed to it by means of 5 bars from 22 to 27 inches long and 3 inches wide laid across the bottom and sunk into the wood in the same way as the longitudinal bars, and having a contrivance somewhat resembling what carpenters call *dove-tailing* to give them a more secure hold of the timber. Each cross-bar was also fixed to the bottom by a wooden bolt at each end. Besides these holes there were five pairs of larger holes $1^{3}/_{4}$ inches in diameter running along the bottom nearly in a line with the bolt holes, but without any apparent connection with the repairs. They are at irregular intervals of from 18 inches to 21 inches apart, and extend from near the stern to $6^{1}/_{2}$ feet from the prow where the last pair are situated. This canoe, after being exhibited at the British Association which met next year at Aberdeen, was removed to Aboyne Castle where it still remains.

The same party that recovered the canoe also brought several beams and logs to land. One of these was 23 feet long, 16½ inches broad, and 13 inches deep. It did not taper, but was hewn to the same dimensions throughout. The corners were generally much worn off as if by the action of water, but in one or two places they were almost entire, and showed that originally the log had been carefully squared. At each end there was a notch or fitting cut out evidently for the purpose of connecting the beam with some other portion of the fabric of which it had formed part. In each of these fittings there were four larger holes which appeared to have been formed by iron tools, and to have been intended for receiving wooden bolts, being very nearly 3 inches in diameter. Besides these, holes of smaller size, generally about 1½ inches in diameter, were scattered over the whole surface of the beam, in some of which the wooden pins or bolts still remained. In no part was there anything found like the mark or remains of an iron bolt or nail. There can be no doubt that the structure of which this beam formed a part was of a very massive character; and indeed so many similar beams have from time to time been recovered that it is believed a new gangway of very considerable proportions might have been constructed from their timber. It is more doubtful whether the bridge of which they formed part was of very ancient date. Judging from the workmanship bestowed on several of the beams, they appeared to have belonged to a structure not earlier than the

16th century, whilst others manifested such a rude state of art as to lead one to believe that they were shaped in very remote times.

One of this description was brought ashore at the time the canoe was found. It was a plank of oak 22½ feet long by about 16 inches of average breadth and of very unequal thickness, varying from 4 inches to a sharp edge. On the sharp edge there were indentations which seemed to have been caused by fire, and several other portions of the plank bore marks of having been charred, suggesting the idea that fire had been used to reduce it to shape. At 8 inches from one of the ends there was a large oval hole, not right through the plank but cut in a slanting direction, and of so irregular a shape that it could scarcely have been formed by an iron boring tool. It was also remarkable that the plank did not present an even surface like a board but one that undulated with the natural bendings of the wood, presenting the idea of its having been split into a plank. One thing was evident, it had neither been sawed nor wrought upon by an iron tool. Several planks of similar shape and manufacture have been at different times dragged from the lake, but none such, so far as I am aware, have ever been observed in the ruined framework of the bridge. I am therefore of opinion that there have been several bridges at different periods. The last is known to have existed to the middle of the 17th century; the first was probably prehistoric.

Although a considerable quantity of timber was obtained from the lake for some time after 1859, the supply was gradually becoming less while the number of visitors and relic-hunters was yearly increasing, till at length the oak of Loch Kinnord, from being applied to such ignoble uses as the roofing of houses and laying the foundations of bridges, had come to be highly prized as material for cabinet-making, and the smaller supply of black oak for conversion into snuff-boxes, walking-sticks, and even paper-cutters; so that now a good, characteristic specimen of the great beams of grey oak once found in such abundance can scarcely be met with in the district.

The last recovery of important relics was made on 10th August, 1875, when Lord and Lady Huntly met the inhabitants of the surrounding district for the purpose of taking to land a canoe, which had previously been discovered by Mr. John Simpson, Meikle Kinnord. Its position was about 80 yards from the north shore, and 200 yards due west from the Castle Island. While the people were engaged in fixing the hauling tackle, they discovered a second canoe very near the same place. But so deeply were they sunk in the mud which had been accumulating over them for ages that the task of bringing them to land was far from easy. Under the skilful directions of Lord Huntly, however, both were brought ashore without the least injury.

These canoes, which are hollowed out of single logs of oak, measure respectively 30 feet 2 inches and 29 feet 3 inches in length. The width of both is somewhat irregular, varying, in the case of the longer, from 3 feet 5 inches at the stern, to 3 feet 7 inches at the centre, and tapering thence to the prow. The other is somewhat wider. The sides - except quite near the prows - are so much worn away that it is impossible to ascertain, with any degree of exactitude, how deep they may have been in their original condition. The thickness of the keels of both is about 7 inches, but they are also much worn away. Each has four ribs or ridges across the bottom at nearly equal distances from each other, apparently the remains of what had once afforded resistance to the feet of the rowers. In respect of shape and construction, though larger in size, they are very similar to the canoe recovered in 1859.

At the same time there were brought to land two large oak beams that had belonged to the bridge, and two smaller coupling beams, one of which was found inserted into a larger beam by means of a mortised hole and fastened by a wooden pin. The largest of these beams was 37 feet in length, had 7 mortised holes, and measured on the sides $15\frac{1}{2}$ by $12\frac{1}{2}$ inches.

Later in the same season another canoe was discovered by a boating party near the smaller, or Prison Island. It appears to be filled with stones, and may have been swamped while conveying its cargo to the island, or intentionally sunk by overloading it with these stones. It has not yet been brought to land. Its position is about 30 yards south-east of the crannog.

OBJECTS OF STONE. - A baptismal font, of mediaeval age, was found near where the chapel stood at Meikle Kinnord. It is formed out of a boulder of rough disintegrating granite, and measures 5 feet $2\frac{1}{2}$ inches in circumference. There is a similar one among the antiquities preserved at the Church of Tullich.

The large sculptured stone which formerly stood on the north shore is referred to at p. 31.

A prehistoric stone ball was found in the underground structure described at the end of this chapter.

Objects of Bronze. - One of the most interesting antiquarian relics was found near the Castle Island by John MacPherson, Bogangore, about 1833. It is a bronze ewer with handle and spout, and stands on three legs. It measures 10½ inches in height, and is evidently an article of domestic use (by general assent it was at once recognised locally as Malcolm Canmore's coffee-pot!).

FIG. 5. - BRONZE VESSEL FROM LOCH KINNORD

When the crannog in the Loch of Leys, Banchory, was explored in 1850, a vessel very similar in general appearance and design was among the relics recovered.

Another interesting bronze object was found in 1874 by Mr. John Simpson, Meikle Kinnord. The summer was dry, and the water being very low, he was one day amusing himself by observing the bottom of the loch as he was being rowed along the south shore, when he caught sight of something that seemed to be artificial sticking upright in the sand. He succeeded in reaching it, and brought it home in a perfectly entire condition; but unfortunately soon after, someone handling it rather incautiously, it was

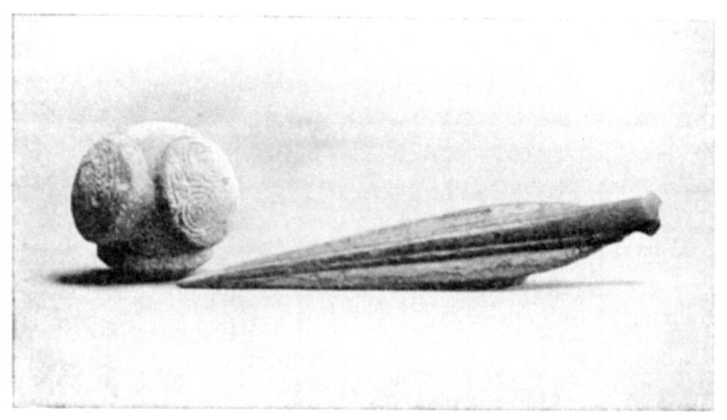

FIG. 6. - BRONZE SPEAR-HEAD FOUND IN LOCH KINNORD

broken in two places. The fragments, however, were carefully re-united so that the weapon might present the exact appearance it had when recovered from the lake. It is a beautiful and highly finished bronze spear-head with a portion of the oak handle remaining in the socket when first discovered. The wood was much decayed, but still retained evidence of having been broken across at the point where it entered the head. The bronze is soft, and, though seemingly not much corroded on the surface, is very brittle and a good deal decayed in the heart. It is far from being so hard or sound in quality as the metal of the bronze vessel - probably it belongs to an earlier age. From the tip to the point where the leaf-shaped sides join the socket it is $12^{1}/_{2}$ inches in length; the extreme breadth is $2^{3}/_{4}$ inches.*

Another bronze spear-head found at Little Kinnord is now in the National Museum, Edinburgh.

Objects of Vitreous Paste. - Specimens of various articles in this material have been frequently found round the shores of the loch. Some of them are obviously beads, others rings, but there are some whose exact purpose it is not possible to make out. That they are meant for ornament is clear. They have been frequently found in crannogs and brochs in other parts of Scotland.

Besides the objects mentioned, it is known that many other relics of antiquity have been found in or on the shores of Loch Kinnord, of which no accurate description can now be obtained. Those which we have described present a fair sample of multitudes of others which have been lost or destroyed.

The Two Islands.

The larger, or Castle Island, is situated about 80 yards from the north shore. The depth of water in the intervening channel is from 5 to 7 feet at the west end, increasing to 10 at the east. About the middle of the loch the depth is 8 feet, decreasing towards the south shore to 4 or 5 feet. The deepest part is between the two islands - 10 feet. It should be remembered, however, that by the operations on the

[*The carved stone ball, which happens to be photographed with the spear-head, was found in the Lumphanan district. It may be compared with the specimen on page 13.]

burn of Dinnet the level formerly stood 2½ or 3 feet higher all over. The island is oval in form and contains about a Scots acre. It was in tillage till 1826, since which time it has been kept under grass. It is evidently natural, and does not appear to be in any marked respect different from the nearest land in the materials of which it is composed. These are mostly water-worn stones of small size, interspersed with a few larger boulders and thinly covered over with coarse gravel and sand. Judging by the eye, the ground, which is pretty level a-top, rises to about 16 feet above the present water level. The stones which line the island beach are, however, considerably larger than those on the land shore, and several of them, notwithstanding a long exposure to the action of the surf, still bear marks of dressing. The site of the castle can be traced in a dry season by the withered grass and vegetation.

The smaller island, or crannog, is wholly artificial. It is situated about 250 yards from the nearest shore and 400 yards to the east of the larger island. The shape is elliptical, 25 by 21 yards, and the ground rises in a conical form to the height of about 8½ feet (see pl. VI, p. 83).

The following note was taken by the author on the occasion of a visit of examination in the year 1859.

"The essential structural feature of this island is the oak piling. The piles are arranged in three rows, one within the other, and planted at the distance of 2½ feet apart, with a framework of horizontal beams interlacing them. They are set almost perpendicularly except on one side, that fronting the largest reach of water, where they incline slightly inwards as if the better to resist the shock of the waves.

This framework surrounds the island on three sides and is guarded in front by a facing of loose stones in the form of a rough causeway. The subjoined draft will give an idea of its nature. The observer is supposed to be looking down on the top of the island. The diagram is of course too regular and mathematically exact, but it will serve to make plain the principles of construction. Most of the horizontal beams have been carried off or washed away, but three are to be

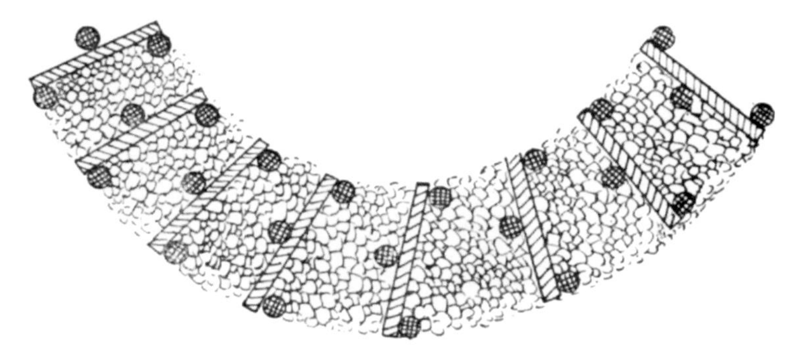

FIG. 7. - PLAN OF A SEGMENT OF THE OUTER CIRCLE OF THE CRANNOG, SHOWING THE ARRANGEMENT OF PILES, BEAMS AND STONES.

seen in position, covered in great part with stones, and a few more are lying about. I removed a few of the stones from those I found in position in order to ascertain the mode of locking. Like the upright piles, these horizontal rafters appear to be strong rough arms of oak trees from 7 to 8 feet in length and about 8 inches in diameter, some more, some less. I observed but one hewn into a regular beam, and it was not *in situ*.

"On the three sides of the island supported by the piles the depth of the water increases very rapidly, and even on that side towards the nearest land the increase in depth though not so sudden is yet much more abrupt than on any part of the land shore or larger island. The space within the palisades is not composed of small stones, sand and gravel like the land shores and larger island, but consists of loose stones averaging from 20 to 30 lbs. in weight, thrown together much in the same way as old cairns were piled. The interstices have been filled up by decayed vegetable matter brought thither by the winds and waves. In this way the seeds of grass and trees found a lodgment and sprang up, till the island no longer wears the aspect of a cold grey cairn, but looks like a thicket on the bosom of the lake with a coating of rank vegetation around the roots of the trees. But the mask is easily torn off; the sward may readily be peeled away by the hand, and then the cairn-like structure of the island beneath becomes obvious. That it was originally a crannog and built at the time when lake-dwellings were the favourite residences of the people, admits of no doubt; but I believe that in later times it may have been enlarged, and used for other purposes than a common human dwelling. Indeed the tradition that it was finally used as the keep or prison of the Castle which stood on the larger island must be accepted as having a foundation in fact; though regarding what changes it may have undergone in the long interval between the time when it first rose by the diligent hands of the lake-dwellers to afford them shelter and security from their enemies to the time when it became a dungeon for human incarceration, torture and death, tradition and history are alike silent, and its own grey stones, and weather-worn piles, with the relics that have been found around it, are now the only witnesses of its vast antiquity."

UNDERGROUND STRUCTURE AT MEIKLE KINNORD.

On the southern margin of the loch there is a peninsula, known by the name of Gardiebane, which bears evident traces of having been once fortified by a moat and rampart, and shows fainter traces of a rampart all round. Before the level of the lake was reduced the water very nearly encircled this place. The ground immediately adjacent has been under cultivation for many years, and no one recollects anything peculiar about the surface before it was brought under the plough, except some traces of a paved way, noticed below.

While a servant was ploughing in this field in 1872, at a spot about 100 yards from the moat of Gardiebane, he felt his plough irons several times graze the surface of a stone, and thinking the sound hollow, he made some investigation, and found that beneath the stone there was a space nearly filled with soft mould. With some assistance from the farm, the stone was removed, and turned out to be a granite slab of an irregular oblong shape, measuring 4 feet 7 inches in medial length and 3 feet in average breadth. It was supported at either end by flat-faced stones set on end and laid together with some care. The space thus enclosed was 3 feet broad at the top, 2 feet at the bottom, and 20 inches deep. This portion was also roughly paved with stones, but there was no pavement in any other part. A stone ball 3 inches in diameter was found among the soil excavated; something resembling a bone was also discovered, but as it crumbled away in the handling, it is doubtful whether it really was one or not. In attempting to remove a second cover the stone was broken; but judging from the fragments it does not appear to have been dressed, but to have been a rough gneiss boulder.

The accompanying plate (from a survey and drawing by Mr. Alexander Ogilvy, communicated by Sir John Clark, Bart., of Tillypronie) shows the ground plan, sections and measurements of this curious structure (see P. 99).

The side walls are composed of a single course of stones set on edge; some of these are placed with some art and apparent care, both as to joints and levelling a-top, but the rest are roughly set side by side. The entire length of the structure is 21 feet; and the broadest part, at the bifurcation, is 3 feet, the passage gradually narrowing towards E, F, where it is only 18 inches wide and 30 inches high ; one of the covers in position at this part is a shapeless block of gneiss (the rock most abundant in the neighbourhood), which probably would weigh a little less than 1½ cwt., *i.e.*, about a fair lift for a man. Under it was found a concave stone in the bottom with the concavity turned upwards. The hollow appears to be the result of the natural cleavage of the block from which it has been obtained. It is in position. Below the large flag, and for some distance (2 or 3 feet) towards D, a quantity of cinders and charred wood was found. The side stones at this part bore marks of the action of fire, but the overlying flag was but slightly stained with smoke.

An old man, who had occupied this piece of land about forty years before, informed me that while trenching a part of it opposite to Gardiebane, he came upon a paved way passing over a small marsh, but that it ceased when the hard ground was reached. Having got him on the spot, I asked him to point out, as nearly as he could recollect, the direction taken by this paved way. He did so without hesitation. The line he indicated fell forty yards or thereabout to the left, or east of the underground structure.

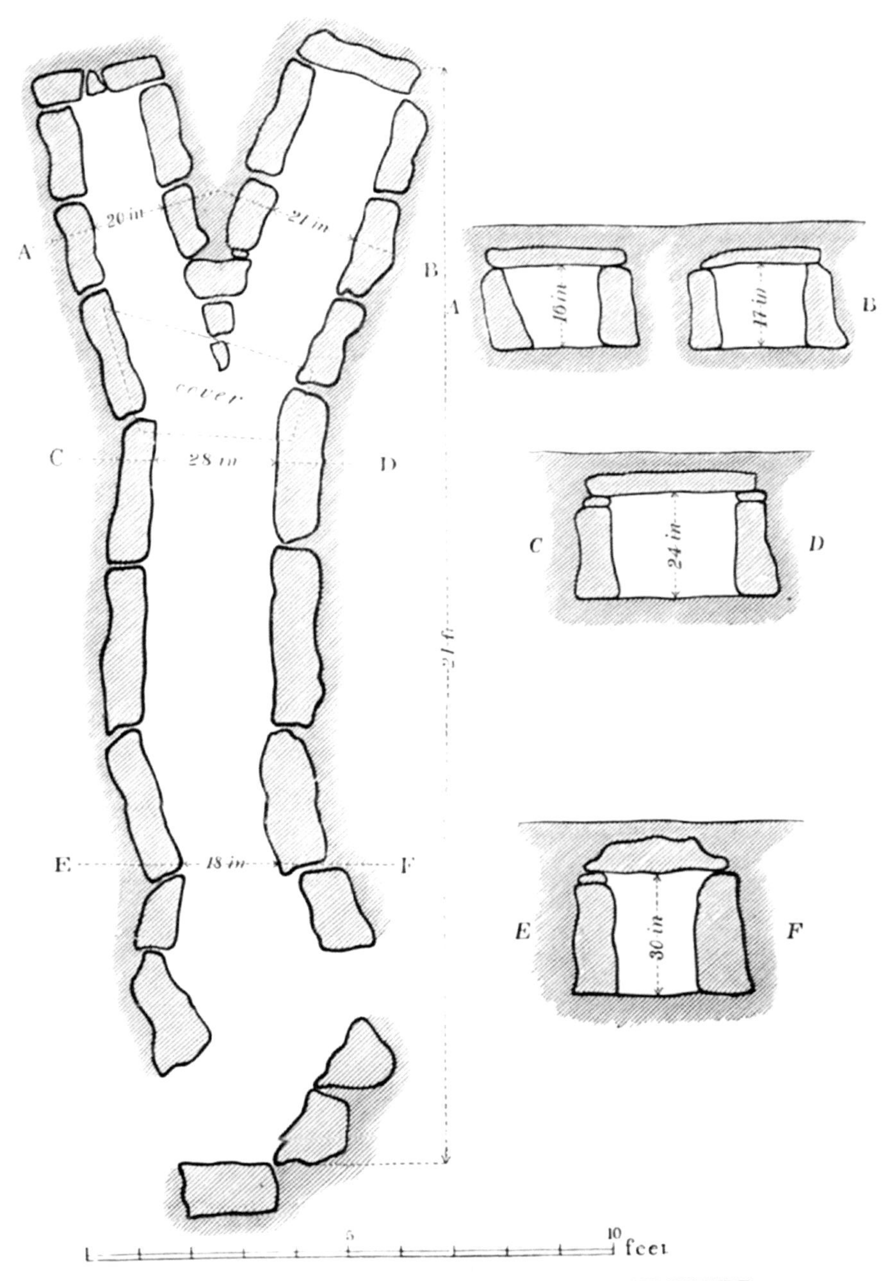

FIG. 8. PLAN AND SECTION OF UNDERGROUND STRUCTURE.

MISCELLANEOUS PAPERS

STORY OF NELLIE OGG

THE following sketch of humble life, as it existed on the shores of Loch Kinnord towards the close of the 18th century, may not be unacceptable to the general reader as a sequel to the foregoing history.

When our story opens, Nellie Ogg was a playful little girl about twelve years of age. Her parents occupied a small croft towards the north-western end of the loch. The blight of desolation, in that dreariest and deepest of all its aspects - when it follows as a reaction on unwonted stir and adventitious populousness - had fallen on the whole district. Gone were the ancient inhabitants with their hill forts, lake crannogs, and their big canoes; gone were the early Christian preachers with their cross-incised stones; gone were the great English armies that had more than once been seen here in their vain attempt to subjugate the stubborn Scottish nation; gone were the excitement and bustle wont to attend the visits of royal personages here; gone were also the pomp and circumstance of the great baronial hall, thronged with the retinue of the high feudal lord who scarcely owned a superior; and gone too were the hordes of Highland banditti, and the relentless soldiers of conquering generals, whose work was plunder and demolition - all were gone, while the wrecks they left behind them were heaps of ruins, a few fragments of blackened walls, and a confused mass of broken and disjointed timbers.

In this state the shores of Loch Kinnord had long lain almost desolate. It was a place of evil fame, haunted by the ghosts of the departed, by the denizens of the nether world and their coadjutors, the wizards and witches of the human kind! Thus superstition had invested it with a terror, which, though it kept the land tenantless, yet for long preserved the ruins from spoliation.*

By and bye one daring sceptic after another ventured to settle on the unoccupied fields, till at length a goodly number of small huts, called "reekan' hooses," again

*As an example of the superstitious beliefs then entertained, it may be stated that the witches, in common with the fraternity elsewhere, rode the air on broomsticks, and the wizards sailed the lake in riddles - *i.e.*, corn-sieves divided into meshes by interlacing splits of wood. One of these wizards had the gifts of music and poetry to so high a degree that his fame had reached the capital, and a great lord there became exceedingly desirous of securing his services. The wizard, however, rejected all offers of such employment made to him; and it was discovered that he could not be compelled unless some greater magician were found to put him under the required spell or bondage. The services of such an one were at length secured, who, coming to Loch Kinnord under disguise, got an interview, and laid his wand upon the shoulder of this preternatural genius, who henceforth for a certain number of years became his bondsman. He now hired him out to the nobleman in Edinburgh, in whose halls he sang his songs, and at whose banquets he supplied the music. But though bound in obedience to the spell upon him to perform his task, he was not happy, for a fragment of his muse, which has survived in the traditions of the district, represents him as frequently thus soliloquizing:-

"I'd rather be on Loch Kinnord
Rowan' in a riddle,
Than in the toon o' Edinburgh
Playan' on the fiddle."

gave signs of human life, though in its humblest forms, in scattered clachans around the lake.

In one of these huts lived Duncan Ogg, and his wife, Tibby Turner, the parents of the subject of our story. Their habitation was humble and their substance small. The former consisted of a *but* and a *ben* affording accommodation respectively to the bestial and the family. There were no outhouses. Indeed to have made such a separation between the rational and irrational members as would have resulted from delegating the latter to outhouses, would have been an infringement on the principles that regulated the establishment, for the bestial were accounted an integral portion of the family circle; at least they were so in little Nellie Ogg's view.

"Cromie," the cow, was so sensible and alive to her duty and station that she knew her place in the family circle and generally kept it, seldom stepping "ben" the house, unless, when unduly excited by female curiosity to see a little of high life, or tempted by appetising odours about baking time; for she dearly loved a bit of oat cakes. But even then she never ventured farther than merely to show her "honest, sonsy face" within the "ben" door. The least commotion within that apartment was sure to bring her to a sense of her duty, and cause her to retreat in some confusion to her own quarters. She was an old servant, and respected the dignity of the family.

Very different was the conduct of the other under-members of the household. These were the three goats, whose names were Jock, Maysie, and Old Jonet. Old Jonet, it must be allowed, had some sense of decorum about her; but as for Jock and Maysie, no discipline would teach them manners. They had been petted and pampered, and allowed such liberties in their early years that they never could be made to understand that when their beards grew they ought to behave differently. And then they were so pert and frolicsome in their ways that it was found impossible not soon to forget their acts of more serious misconduct, and fall a-petting them again. In fact, had they been human creatures they would have been entirely spoiled, and would have behaved not one whit better than they did in their brute capacity.

They lost no opportunity of stealing "ben" the house, and were not at all particular about appropriating what they found that suited their tastes, whether it were the cakes on the table, or the cold porridge set apart for the goodman's supper, when he should come in at even; and if detected by Nellie they looked so innocent of any wrong-doing that her wrath soon fell. She would scold and threaten, generally winding up with, "Ah, Jock, Jock, ye'll catch it, my man, when mammie comes in." Should mammie then come in, a storm was sure to burst on the head of Jock in the shape of a severe cuffing; and then Nellie never failed to take his part, throwing her arms about his neck, and bemoaning his castigation - "Peer man! ye'll nae dee the like again; noo will ye, Jock?" If the cuffing had been unusually severe, Jock generally shed some tears at this commiseration, which mark of penitence Nellie was not slow to plead in his favour - "Oh, mammie! I kent he widna dee't again; see, he's greetan'." If the storm was not yet over, Tibby Turner would angrily answer - "Lat him greet there, the scoun'rel; I canna turn my fit about but he's sure to be in some bad ploy or ither." Seeing wrath still in store,

Nellie would take hold of his horn and lead him away from further danger, saying in a coaxing tone, "Come awa' but the house, Jockie, mammie's angry; but ye'll nae dee't again, noo will ye?" and then the two would disappear.

Thus within doors Nellie's management of the little herd was often interfered with; abroad, however, it was supreme, and there it must be allowed, there was less ground to complain of the misconduct of any member of it. Nellie, in short, was goat-herd, and considered the three as peculiarly under her protection. Not only did they look to her for guidance in all matters, but by some rule of goat-life they kept their respective stations among themselves. The leadership was so absolutely in the hands of Jock that on no occasion would either of the other two presume to march without having him as vanguard. Maysie, it is true, was always by his side, and usually only a neck behind, while Old Jonet brought up the rear. Should, by any chance, men or dogs disturb this order of march, there was no peace till it was again restored. If hunted, Maysie would wheel round, bleat, and stamp the ground with all fours until she gained her wonted position close by the side of, but a neck behind her leader, where she would boldly join him in offering defiance to all foes. In these times of danger Jonet kept close in the rear, though at other times she allowed herself a considerable latitude of movement.

The Castle Island was their pasture ground. It was then so encumbered with the mouldering *debris* of its former buildings that goats alone could safely pasture among the ruins. The access was over the remains of the old drawbridge, then an unsightly mass of spars and beams. Nellie, who was agile and sure of foot as any of her own goats, had been so long accustomed, evening and morning, to make her way through the labyrinth of timbers, pacing carefully along a spar here, bounding more freely along a plank there, now crosswise, now forward, zig-zagging her way from mainland to island and back again, that it was believed she would not have missed a foot had she been blindfolded.

Poor Nellie! One morning the goats were led forth by her father and conducted to the end of the drawbridge. Arrived there, he tried hard to make them take the planks; but in vain. They had been accustomed to be led, and would not be driven. As far as he judged it safe he walked on before them, talking to them as his daughter had been wont to do; but it was not the shepherd's voice, and they would not follow. That day, nor for many days thereafter, the goats went not to the Castle Island.

And where was Nellie? At home abed, and very, very sick. Days passed, and she became worse. At length some fiery red spots on her brow disclosed her malady. It was small-pox. From the attack, which was a severe one, she barely escaped with her life. Her young and vigorous constitution alone brought her through it; but though her step at length regained its firmness and her voice its tone, her cheek had for ever lost its colour and her eye its lustre. Poor Nellie was blind. From the day she fell sick to the day she was able to walk abroad again no attempt had been made to force the goats across the old drawbridge; but in the wanderings of her mind, when the hot fever was on her brain, she kept up an almost continuous conversation with Jock, Maysie, and Old Jonet, as in imagination she led them to and from the island along the well-remembered planks of the ruined fabric of confused timbers, warning them of danger here, and of some sharp turn requiring caution there.

Soon after her restoration to health she insisted on resuming her former charge. To humour her she was allowed to be with them about the doors; but for some time she was not permitted to follow them out of sight of her mother. Seeing how well she managed and how guarded she was whenever she ventured on unfamiliar ground, a less strict watch was by and bye kept over her movements. One day when she had been absent beyond her usual time, her mother went out to see what had become of her. Terror-stricken she beheld her blind child walking along the narrowest plank near the middle of the drawbridge, followed by Jock, Maysie, and Old Jonet, in the old established order. The mother saw no more, for covering her face with her hands that she might not behold her child perish, she sank on the ground in a sort of stupor. Nellie and her charge had been to the island and were now returning; and ere the mother had recovered from her fright, they were all safe on the mainland. Nellie was severely reprimanded for her thoughtless daring; but she still maintained she could tread the planks as securely and as safely as ever she had done; and though it was long before she received her parents' permission to venture on the bridge again, it was not long till she rightly interpreted the bleating of Jock to mean, "Oh, bring us to the island, Nellie"; and Nellie had not the heart to refuse him.

So for many years blind Nellie Ogg conducted her father's goats to and from the Castle Island along the planks of the ruined drawbridge. Hers was the last foot that ever crossed it.

At length a fearful gale swept the middle plank into the lake, and Nellie's vocation was ended. She was alive, it is said, though very old and frail, when in 1808 the workmen of the famous engineer, Telford, pillaged the drawbridge for timbers to lay the foundations of his new stone bridge over the Dee at Ballater.

Pl. VII.

TULLICH CHURCH

THE CHURCH OF TULLICH

THERE are few more interesting ecclesiastical ruins on Deeside than those of the old Church of Tullich. The site commands one of the finest views in the district. In the foreground of the landscape, looking westward, is the broad valley on which Ballater now stands, with the silver Dee winding through it, flanked on the one hand by the rugged front of Pannanich hill, and on the other by the rocky wood-clad steeps of Craigandarroch, while a little further to the right the romantic Pass of Ballater, like a rift in an amphitheatre of enclosing mountains, seems to offer the only approach to the regions beyond. The opening to the left is the sylvan valley of the Muick, seemingly shut in by the picturesque Coyle hills whose conical summits, overtopped by the "Steep frowning glories of dark Loch na Garr" form the background of the magnificent scene. It is worthy of observation that, in Aberdeenshire and over the north of Scotland generally, the selection of sites for our earliest Christian ecclesiastical institutions was made by men who had an intuitive appreciation of the picturesque in nature. The sites of Tullich Church, and of Coldstone in Cromar, and several others in the district are striking evidences of this fact. Our very ancient forefathers were not so devoid of an appreciation of the beautiful in nature and in art as we are sometimes apt to suppose. When we reflect that there is in the old churchyard of Coldstone a small sculptured stone with an incised cross on it of remarkable beauty, which the late Dr. Joseph Robertson pronounced to belong to the 8th or early part of the 9th century, and that there is in the churchyard of Tullich an almost exactly similar stone with similarly carved cross, we can hardly avoid the conclusion that at even this early date the Christian missionaries - disciples of St. Columba - were men of cultured minds and refined tastes. But we might even go beyond this in claiming such mental or artistic endowments for our remote ancestors. It is a well established fact, of which the old churchyard of Tullich is one of the most striking examples, that our earliest Christian missionaries, for politic as for other purposes, adopted the sites of the ancient heathen worship as the places where the early Christian rites were to be observed. And if so, we cannot avoid the inference that even our heathen ancestors, before the sixth century, were endowed with an eye for the picturesque and the beautiful in nature.

Be this as it may, there is no denying the fact that our earliest Christian establishments were placed in the most picturesque situations which the district in which they are located could command.

Notwithstanding its fine situation and romantic surroundings, the documentary history of the Church of Tullich is rather meagre. The name of its founder, however, St. Nachalan or Nathalan, is preserved in *Tullinathlak*, the old name of the church and parish, and if he does not figure in authentic history, his legendary renown is well-established on Deeside. In Forbes's "Kalendars of Scottish Saints" we have the story of Nachalan as given in the "Aberdeen Breviary." "He is believed to have been born in the northern parts of the Scoti, in ancient times, at Tullicht, in the diocese of Aberdeen, a man of great sanctity and devotion, who, after he had come to man's estate and been imbued with the liberal arts, devoted himself and his wholly to divine contemplation."

"And when he learned that among the works of men's hands the cultivation of the earth approached nearest to divine contemplation, though educated in a noble family, with his own hands he practised the lowly art of cultivating the fields, abandoning all other occupations, that he might employ his mind, so as never to give place to the contagion of the base solicitations of the flesh. Meanwhile, as he warred his warfare against the devil and the perishing world, a terrible famine broke out among his neighbours, relations, and friends, so that almost the whole people were in danger of perishing by hunger and want of food. But God's saint, Nathalan, moved by the greatest piety, distributed all his grain, for the name of Christ, to the poor. But when the time of spring came, when all green things are committed to the bowels of the earth, not having ought to sow in the land which he cultivated with his own hands, by divine revelation he ordered it all to be strewn and sown with sand, from which sand a great crop of all kinds of grain grew up and was greatly multiplied."

"But in the time of harvest, when a multitude of both sexes were collected by him to gather in the crop, a great tempest of rain was sent forth, so that these husbandmen and women were forced to abstain from labour. Therefore he, excited by anger, along with the other reapers, murmured a little against God. But on the tempest straightway ceasing, feeling that he had offended Him, induced by penitence, he bound his right hand to his leg with an iron lock and key, and forthwith threw the key into the river Dee, making a solemn vow that he would never unlock it until he had visited the threshold of the blessed apostles Peter and Paul, which actually took place."

"Having entered the city [of Rome], approaching in meditation the monuments of the saints which are there on every side, and bewailing his sin, he adored that Creator whom he had heretofore offended. As he went through the most remarkable places of the city, he met a naked boy carrying a little fish for sale, which he purchased at a low price. By the divine power he found in its belly the key, unrusted, which he had flung into the Dee, and with it he opened the lock upon his leg. But the Supreme Pontiff, informed of this mighty wonder, and summoning him as a man of superior sanctity into his presence, made him in spite of his reluctance a bishop."

"Rendering himself for many years acceptable to all in the practice of divine contemplation in Rome, not forgetful to extreme old age of his native soil, by permission of the Roman Pontiff he returned to that part of Scotland whence he sprung. Having built the Churches of Tullicht, Bothelim, and Colle, at his own expense, he dedicated them to Almighty God, and they actually exist in these provinces, dedicated to his honour."

The story of Nachalan is still commemorated in two of the place-names of the district. The pool near the church into which he threw the key is known as the Key Pool, Gaelic *Poll na h-iuchrach*, of which the English is a translation. The version of the first part of the legend commonly current in the Gaelic speaking districts of Deeside, is slightly different from that of the Breviary. When spring and seed-time came round, after a winter of famine, the country people found that they had nothing wherewith to sow their fields, and came to Nachalan in their extremity. He bade them sow as usual, but with sand from the river instead of grain; and this having been duly done, he went to the fields, and prayed, and blessed them. Hence the origin of the name Sluievannachie, near Ballater, the place where the miracle of reaping corn after sand is said to have happened. The Gaelic is Sliabh Bheannachaidh (pronounced Slioo-vyannachy), "moor of blessing." Near by, in Glenmuick, there is also a Dalmallachy, which is apparently Dail Mallachaidh, "haugh of cursing," and probably implies another Nachalan legend, though, if this is so, it has been lost to tradition.

The saint was believed to have been buried at Tullich, and up to the Reformation the sick and infirm resorted to his grave owing to its high reputation for miraculous efficacy in the cure of disease. We may digress for a moment to notice that another of Nachalan's foundations, the Church of Bethelny (now Old Meldrum), also claimed to be the resting-place of the saint's body, and from an account of the parish written in 1724 we learn that "all the people observe Saint Nachalan's day as a great holyday, giving themselves up entirely to mirth and jollity, because the last time the plague was in Scotland, though it raged in all the parishes about, yet it did not enter into that parish at all, which the common people impute to his being buried there."

Up till recently there stood a sculptured cross on a rude block of granite some distance to the east of the churchyard of Tullich. It was popularly designated St. Nachalan's cross. Whether it had any connection with him may be doubtful. It has now irrecoverably disappeared, having been broken up by the vandal hands of the road contractor in 1857, and its material converted into road metal. Such is the miserable fate that has overtaken many of our most ancient monuments.

The historical fact which may safely be inferred from these legends, and their very early prevalence, is that the light of Christianity was introduced into these parts by Nachalan, one of the band of missionaries from the southwest, who, with Columba as pioneer and leader, laboured among the Northern Picts. What his exact date may have been it is impossible to say, but probably it lay some time in the 7th century, or possibly even as early as the 6th.

The earliest documentary reference to the church and parish of Tullich is contained in Bagimont's Taxt Roll of Benefices within the Kingdom of Scotland, wherein *Tullinathlak* is represented as one of the four churches within the diocese of Aberdeen that were under the patronage of the Knights Templars. This Roll refers to the ecclesiastical condition of Scotland towards the close of the 13th century. There still remain some traces, though faint, of the occupation of the Knights Templars. Although the surrounding lands have been for ages reclaimed from the waste, the circumvallation can still be discerned, and portions of the moat are often flooded in winter storms. After the disappearance of the Templars the patronage of Tullich became vested in the Earls of Mar, who assigned the tithes, or at least a portion of them, to the Canons of the Cathedral Church of Aberdeen, who took some share in providing for the supply of ordinances. This arrangement continued down to the time of the Reformation.

After the Reformation a few scanty facts emerge into light regarding the ecclesiastical history of Tullich. It is well known the sudden overthrow of the old faith found the Reformers inadequately supplied with Protestant ministers to fill the places of the Roman Catholic priests. This was especially true in the north where Protestantism was practically forced on the people, from the south. Accordingly we find that about 1574 for the seven churches of Crathie, Glenmuick, Abergairn, Tullich, Glentanar, Aboyne, and Birse there was only one superintendent minister, the parishioners at most of these places having to be content with a resident "reader" or "exhorter." Lawrence Cowtiss (we may presume from the name that he was a local man) was reader from 1567 to 1580. By 1599 the position of matters had somewhat improved, as in that year John Leslie, formerly of Slains, was appointed minister of Glenmuick, Tullich, and Abergairn, which office he held till 1623, when he was deprived by the Bishop. Various "readers" are mentioned (see Scott's *Fasti*) for the neighbouring parishes during those years of transition. During the 17th and 18th centuries Tullich shared with Glenmuick and Glengairn the services of one minister, the practice being to preach in the three churches in rotation. In 1798 a new central church was erected on the moor of Ballater, and apparently the building at Tullich was allowed to fall into neglect.

The remains of the fabric, even in their fragmentary condition, are of considerable interest, as parts are believed to date from the 15th century. But the archaeologist will no doubt find more to engage his attention in the splendid series of sculptured stones which, when their message is duly interpreted, carry back the story of this ecclesiastical establishment to its foundation and even earlier (see plate VIII).

FIG. 9. - STONE A, ON PLATE VIII OPPOSITE (FROM A RUBBING)

And first as to the monument marked A. I discovered this stone in 1866, when I took a rough sketch of it. Some years afterwards I drew the Earl of Southesk's attention to it, he being keenly interested in the problems of our early sculptured stones. The slab then served as the inside lintel of a blind door-way that had been built up when the church was last repaired, and was partly concealed by the walls. It is needless to ask what the figures symbolise. They are of the character usually found on sculptured stones which are by some regarded as being pre-Christian, and have formed the subject of much learned disquisition and conjecture without leading to any very satisfactory

Pl. VIII. A B C

SCULPTURED STONES AT TULLICH

conclusion. The subject is a large one and cannot be entered upon at this place. The Earl of Southesk's work, *Origins of Pictish Symbolism*, Edinburgh, 1893, is one of the latest attempts to deal with it, but his conclusions have by no means won general acceptance.* It is to be observed that the slab on which the figures are incised does not belong to any rock found in the neighbourhood, but is a slab of hornblendic schist, the nearest locality of which, so far as I know, is on the hill of Corrennie, 25 miles distant. This fact, as well as the character of the sculpturing, would seem to indicate that even at this early date (probably in the first centuries of our era) our remote ancestors were prepared to put themselves to some considerable trouble to procure proper material on which to engrave these interesting symbols of what they doubtless considered of the highest importance in their religious or political life.

Stone B. - The sculpturing here is in the form of an Iona Cross. The slab, so far as can be ascertained, had formed the outside lintel of a door-way on the south side of the church, and must have been placed there before the Reformation, as the masonry surrounding it belongs to a date anterior to the changes that were made at that period. It had been shaped, without regard to its sculpturing, for some utilitarian purpose, in consequence of which the original form of the stone is now incomplete. The era to which it may be referred is a wide one, extending from the beginning of the 7th century to the end of the 12th or even later. There are strong reasons, however, for assigning it to a very early date in this obscure

[*See note on the "Sculptured Stones" at the end.]

portion of our history. The form of the cross and the character of the sculpturing point to the early period of the Celtic Church.

Stone C. - This bears an imperfectly incised cross, not essentially different in general appearance from that on the previous stone. At one time I regarded the sculpturing on this slab as proving its date to have been not long anterior to Reformation times. On further consideration, however, I am disposed to class B and C more closely together. C, I believe, to be considerably later, but that it cannot be assigned to the centuries immediately preceding the Reformation is, I think, clear. The cross is cut on a large slab of granite of the quality generally found in the neighbourhood, measuring 5 feet 10 inches by 1 foot 8 inches (A and B are a few inches less in length and breadth). The surface has undergone no dressing, nor is there any mark of a tool on the slab other than the lines forming the outline of the cross. The block is rectangular in shape. Whether it was thought sufficient to have it so shaped in the rude manner in which it now appears, or was left in an unfinished condition, cannot now be ascertained. Certain it is that on any supposition the sculpturing is far inferior to that on either of the two more ancient stones.

I was led to its discovery in the following way. While examining the ruins of the church in 1878, my attention was attracted to a large slab (the edge of which only was visible) different in size and shape from the other materials of which the inside half of the dry stone wall forming the south side of the church was composed.

There was no window, door, or recess of any kind to which it could form a lintel. With some difficulty I got to the top of the wall, and succeeded with the aid of a friend in clearing away the superincumbent portion, when I discovered the incised cross on the upper surface. The stone had been placed in the wall simply because it supplied handy material for making it up. It was for a very different purpose it was originally intended. Its position was 9 feet above the ground, and 2 feet from the top of the wall; so that it was very inaccessible, and its removal very desirable.

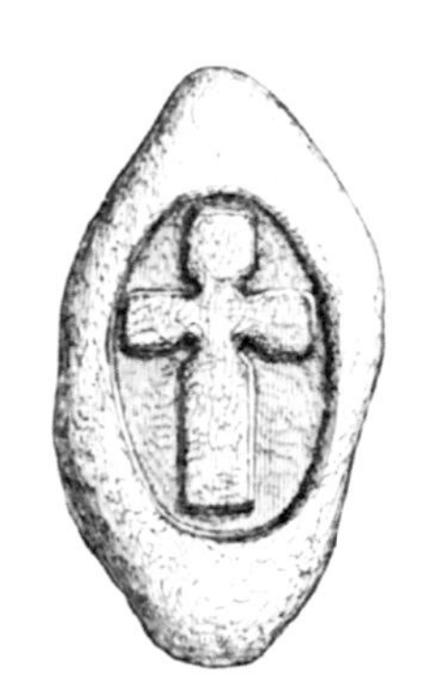

FIG. 10.
EARLY CELTIC CROSS
AT LOGIE-COLDSTONE

I accordingly communicated the discovery to Colonel Farquharson of Invercauld, to whom belonged the right to allow anyone to interfere with the ruins, and not only obtained his permission to do what I thought necessary for the preservation of sculptured stones, while at the same time making them readily available for the inspection of visitors, but he also defrayed the expenses connected with their removal and protection in their present position. They now stand against the north wall of the church on either side of the fine old doorway, the mullions of which, it is to be regretted, being of freestone, are rapidly scaling off. Mr. Jervise assigned the date of the erection of this doorway to the 15th century. The space, which is sufficient to receive any other relics of antiquity that may be discovered in or around the church, is fenced with a railing with lock and key. Already several such relics have found a place within it; among others a small sculptured stone, probably of the 8th or 9th century, and a baptismal font which is of great age and exactly similar to another found near the site of the old chapel at Loch Kinnord, and now deposited within the enclosure of what was once the Museum there.

From the above account we see that the oldest of these stones leads us back to the far distant past, before St. Columba in the west and north or St. Ninian in the south had brought the light of the Gospel into ancient Alban. The whole country was then inhabited by a race Celtic in origin and similar in character, manners, and religion, for the same heathen or pre-Christian symbols are found on the sculptured stones in all parts of the kingdom, and are now recognised as products of ancient Pictavian art. But in as much as these sculptured stones are more abundant in the north, and especially in the north-east, comprising the modern counties of Angus, Mearns, Aberdeen, and Banff, it is not unreasonable to suppose that this territory formed, as it were, the head-quarters of the dominant sept or tribe at that time. It may further be conjectured, judging from the artistic character of the engraving on the Tullich stone that the cultivation of art even at that early date was of no mean order, and that it prevailed over the whole region from the seaboard to the innermost habitable recesses of the country.

With the arrival of the Christian missionary, St. Nachalan or another, a new era begins. Wherever the disciples and followers of St. Columba founded a principal place of worship for their converts, there they raised the symbol of the new religion by a stone with their own peculiar form of cross engraved on it. This cross was at first of the simplest character, an outline only being incised as on those at Tullich and at Coldstone (see p. 121). Afterwards they became more ornamental like the Kinnord and Migvie stones (see pp. 31 and 64), still, however, retaining the distinctive feature of the Iona cross.

WILLIAM MACPHERSON

(1882)

MANY of the antiquaries, tourists, and other excursionists who annually visit the sweet shore and islets of Loch Kinnord, will hear with regret of the death of William MacPherson, Bogangore. This singular man was not only a collector of relics of antiquity in a locality peculiarly rich in archaeological remains, but was himself a specimen of human character, now antiquated, if not extinct, among our Scottish peasantry. Being such a representative "of the days of other years," a short sketch of William's life may have some value to the many who have seen him, and be of interest to the more limited number who can see in it the picture of a state of society now almost forgotten.

William first saw the light in a humble cot in Glencarvy, a secluded tributary of Highland Don, in the spring of 1799. His father occupied a small croft, and also pursued the calling of a carpenter or wheelwright. William's first experiences of life were those of poverty and hardship. Being of a strong and healthy constitution, these trials he quite disregarded while his boyhood lasted, and care was absent. The eldest of a family of three sons and one daughter, he, however, soon began to feel that he must share with his parents the family charges. He therefore betook himself to learn the handicraft his father followed, and which was the mainstay of the family. Hard times came on when he had barely entered his teens. William's recollections of the years 1811-12 were very vivid. "Oor father," he was in the way of saying, "gaed to the south wi' mony mair fae the glens to buy meal an' bran; an' little siller they had to dee't wi', an' we hed to mak' it gang as far as we cud fan it was brocht hame. I min' in the spring o' Eighteen-twal me an' my brithers, little loonies, ga'an oot i' the gloamin', an' wi' the meenlicht, to gaither muggarts an' skellock on the fairms. Nae that we needit to tak that time till't, for the fairmers wudna hae hinder't us in braid daylicht; but we war asham't to lat it be kent that we war so ill aff. I hed begun as early as this to work amo' guns, an' took a shot noo an' than. There war nae restrictions at that time, an' it was consider't in nae wise wrang. Than there cam' ither ill years, the Saxteen an' Seventeen, an' gin it hedna been for oor fishin' and fowlin' at that time, I think we wud hae deet o' starvation. The Twenty-ane an' Twenty-twa warna muckle better, an' we war aften oot wi' the gun an' the rod; but oor principal business was in makin' bowies an' barrels for the smugglers, an' mendin' their black pots. We made little or nae money. I have aften gaen up Glen Noughty an' doon Glen Ernan to see what I cud get for oor wark, an' come hame wi' a teem aneuch pouch but aye wi' a fu' aneuch belly; for the folk hed plenty o' ale but little siller, an' they were willin' to gie fat they hed. I never tried but twice the cadgin' [conveying to market] o' whisky. It was in the year 1823. Gillespie was on the road, an' I set the best pistols I hed in order. It was God's mercy I didna meet him, or I wud hae pistolled him, an' syne I micht hae been hung, like my frien' at Banff."

From a very early date, as indicated, poaching and fishing were his foibles - "black fishing" it was; and with a wholesome contempt for the effeminacy which would eschew such trying exploits, he would narrate with gusto how when "we war young," he had as one of a party, with torch and leister, waded thigh-deep in the Upper Don for miles, when the floating ice was ever and anon grating on his "hinches" with rude shock. His fondness for the chase, though it may have originated in necessity, naturally led to strained relations with the laird. As a specimen of the amenities that sometimes passed between them, we have heard the following story. On one occasion the laird was out hunting, and his dogs happened to kill a hare within sight of the MacPhersons' house. William's dog, which had been watching the sport, at this point found the temptation irresistible, dashed forward, and seized the game under the nose of the laird himself. In high wrath he strode over to where William was standing, and delivered his mind at large on his tenant's present and past misdemeanours - which castigation the young man took in silence, till the laird wound up with the threat that if ever he heard of his dog being after game again he would come and shoot it. "When ye come to shoot my dog," said William, doubtless in the level, impassive tones in which he habitually spoke and which no excitement could vary or disturb, "When ye come to shoot my dog, ye'll better bring your coffin wi' ye than, for ye'll need it to gae hame in." This was a footing for landlord and tenant to stand on!

Presently we hear without surprise that the family, which now consisted of mother and three sons, had no choice but leave their native glen. As William climbed the hillside, moving southward, and before he had lost sight of the spot he knew so well, the evicted poacher - as he would tell those who had got fairly into his confidence - faced round, knelt down "on his bare knees," and uttered a prayer very much of the imprecatory stamp, which included a petition to the effect that he might live to see the time when none of the name or lineage of the man who had forced his family out might be possessors of Candacraig. "An' I *did* live to see't, man," was the usual comment, relative to the petition referred to, with which he concluded, and which it may be added was not the harshest of the petitions bearing on the laird's future fate understood to have been uttered by William on the occasion of bidding farewell to his native glen.

It was in 1825 that the MacPhersons had to leave Donside. They found a temporary shelter in a hut covered with divots at Carlochy, on the shore of Loch Kinnord close to the farm of Meikle Kinnord. Their poverty was so great that, as William used to tell, they lived for some time on nothing but "cauld steer" (oatmeal and water). Meantime the brothers worked hard at any employment that might offer, principally "floating" timber on the Dee, and before long they were able to build a house at Bogangore, on the north-west side of loch, where they set up their lares and penates for good. The management of the croft was attended to by William's brothers - the last of whom, John, a man of quiet and gentle disposition, died a few years ago - while he applied himself to mechanical pursuits.

Attached to his cottage, and built by himself, was a combined wright's shop and smithy. In the mechanical phase of him, William MacPherson was a man of remarkable faculty. The quick, steady eye, and shapely hand with its long tapering fingers, bespoke the born artificer. He could handle his tools deftly in working iron as well as wood; and had his opportunities been greater he would no doubt have exhibited high constructive capacity. As it was, in addition to other work of the kind ordinarily undertaken by the "wricht," he was skilled in the making of musical instruments - as fiddles and pipes of all sorts, and could perform on all or most of those he had occasion to take through hand.

The leading speciality, on account of which William became known to visitors to the locality, was his reputation as a collector of old relics. It was only after he came to Deeside that he applied himself to this pursuit. Guns and pistols of ancient date, swords, Highland dirks, and powder-horns he had, and some of them of considerable interest and value, as well as a sample of the "lang kail gullie," spoken of by Burns, and several implements of the stone period found near by. His most valuable possession in this way, however, was a very handsome bronze pot of the Roman period, which was his brother's "find," it having been discovered by him embedded in the mud on the margin of Loch Kinnord a good many years ago. This very interesting historical relic, which has been figured in the proceedings of the Society of Antiquaries, William guarded with jealous care, resisting the idea of parting with it even at a very tempting price; and we understand he destined it to go at his death to his generous landlord, the Marquis of Huntly.*

With his veneration for the things of antiquity, William combined a peculiarly hearty contempt for what he regarded as modern shams and innovations - improved guns, fishing-rods, even modern music, as compared with the old, stood nowhere. But indeed the range of his censure and suspicion in this regard was comprehensive enough to embrace not a few of our most deeply cherished institutions. In banks and bank notes, for example, his faith was of the slenderest. He distinctly preferred that the savings of his lifetime should be deposited in good solid coin, of silver and gold, in the locker of his own trusty "kist," and guarded against all and sundry by the strength of his own right arm.

Not only was the household at Bogangore noted for the quaint, old-fashioned ways and marked individuality of character that ruled there, but it was amusing to observe that even the animals of the establishment were also in their own way originals. Probably this was due to the kindly, "couthie" intimacy that existed between the masters and their four-footed dependents, whereby the behaviour and habits of the latter acquired something of almost human cast. The dog learnt the art of catching trout in the burn, and regularly brought home his captures. The cow had developed a partiality for the toothsome peewit's egg, and in the spring-time ranged the ground in search of this delicacy. At the proper season the horse paid careful attention to the apple trees, and when the supplies of fallen fruit failed him he might be observed wistfully eyeing the

[*See fig. 5, p. 90,]

branches in a ludicrously human manner. Most curious perhaps of all, the sheep sometimes abandoned their native habitat - though in this case the *res angusta domi* may partly have been the motive - and took to swimming in the loch after aquatic vegetation.

No sketch, even in the briefest outline, of the chief features of William's character would be complete without some reference to the strong hold which old "frets" and superstitions had on his imagination. Like most of the young people in his day and district, he was brought up to regard the reality of witches and warlocks, evil eye, unlucky times and persons, etc., with the same certainty as any other fact of human knowledge. By the time he reached middle age the modern spirit had done its work on most of these and suchlike superstitions, but it failed in his case to shake his hearty belief in them in the slightest degree. At night he habitually walked at the side of the road to be sure to give the witches room to pass; if a beast was ill, the chances were it was bewitched; if a "kittle" piece of work broke or went wrong, he knew (though he mightn't perhaps tell) who had the blame of it. The occult and the supernatural pervaded everything. Such a creed must have been a heavy burden to timorous natures, but it sat lightly on William. He believed and did *not* tremble, marching forward in a dogged, manful manner, though by no means disdaining to take the necessary and approved precautions against the wiles of the enemy.

Born and bred in the Highlands of Strathdon, William preserved a good deal of the old clan feeling among the other archaic traits of his personality. Curiously - perhaps some would say, significantly - enough, the MacPherson, of all the chiefs and great men of the clan, who appealed most to his feelings, was none other than the famous gipsy-cateran, James, immortalised by Burns in his "MacPherson's Rant," who was hanged at Banff about the year 1700. William's admiration for this hero was boundless, and his name was constantly on his lips, as for instance in the conversation given above when he refers to Gillespie. We have heard that he once made a pilgrimage to Banff for the purpose of visiting the scene and rehearsing in his mind on the spot all the incidents of the final act in the MacPherson drama. The cateran's sword - or at least the weapon which passes for such, and which he readily accepted as authentic - he inspected with reverence, and we believe would willingly have exchanged his entire collection of antiquities for this one item.

Until bent down by the weight of years William MacPherson was a man of stalwart figure and form; and his distinctly marked features and firm-set mouth at once gave the impression of a character of great strength and force. His view point was purely and wholly that of the man who, starting in sympathy with the old rude life of the poacher and smuggler of the past times, had kept tenaciously to his own lines of thought and feeling. Yet withal, his range of inquiry and criticism was, in its own way, of the freest and most independent. He had read his Bible and formed his own conclusions on the historical parts of it, at least; but, as he would tell the speculative visitor, he had read the Koran too, and found something good there as well. Thus far had the wheelwright of Bogangore, in his own untutored way, gone in his study of "comparative religion"; and he had even made himself acquainted with the atheistical arguments of Tom Paine in his early time. It only remains to say that, under what seemed a somewhat rough exterior to those who knew him not, William MacPherson retained not only a sturdy sense of right and honour, but a much larger share of considerate forethought and kindliness than many would have given him credit for. Under the sense of failing strength he had been for a considerable period looking forward to the time of his departure; and with characteristic decision and composure had taken care to order his affairs, and make his wishes fully known, in view of that event. Keeping in view the outstanding features of his very distinctive character, and the changed conditions of society into which he had lived without being in almost the least affected thereby in his habits or life or mental conceptions, it might safely be said of the old wheelwright of Bogangore -

"He was a man, take him for all in all,
I shall not look upon his like again."

PREHISTORIC REMAINS AT MULLOCH

THE hill of Mulloch is situated two miles north-east of Dinnet station on the Deeside railway. It is an abrupt and precipitous eminence rising to the height of 900 feet above sea-level and 300 feet above the flat below. Its summit is crowned by a cairn 56 yards in circumference. There are no upright stones now in position, but the foundations of what was probably a hill-fort can easily be traced. The stones are not of large size and are of the granitic rock of which the hill is composed. To the north-east of the large cairn there is another, 35 yards in circumference, with a distinct wall or rather a line of stones surrounding it, measuring 13 yards in diameter. The peculiarity in the structure is that the stones employed are mostly all small, such as could be carried in the hand, like those called "land gatherings" in these parts, that is from 8 to 20 lbs. or thereby. It may also be observed that the surface of the ground around appears as if it had been cleared of such stones. In the close vicinity of this cairn there are four great circular foundations and a large number of small stone mounds. Although these have been in some instances examined, no remains of an archaeological kind have been found in them.

In excavating the cairn of small stones, however, I came upon a stone cist situated in the very centre of the pile. The accompanying illustration will give an idea of its form and dimensions.

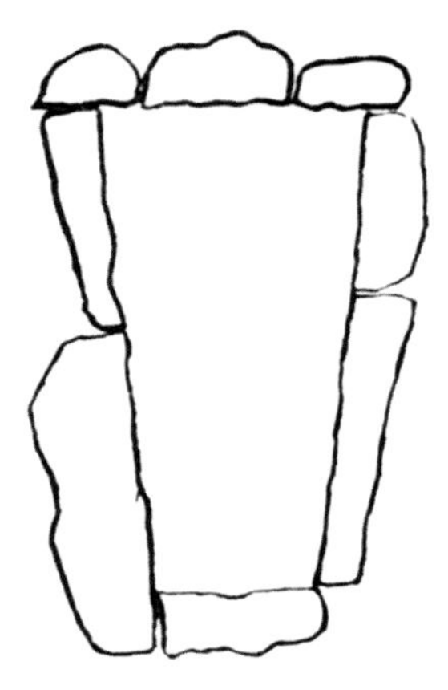

FIG. II. - STONE CIST FOUND IN CAIRN ON MULLOCH

The length of the chamber was 3 feet 3 inches; the breadth at one end 20 inches, and at the other 14; the depth was about 2 feet, but the slabs composing the sides were not all of exactly the same height. Ten slabs in all had been used in its construction, including the two serving for covers. One of these was somewhat fretted and darkened at one end, as if it had been subjected to the action of fire, but this might be due to disintegration, the stone being a decomposing granite. The floor of the chamber was not formed of slabs, but consisted of the natural gravel, which was reached after removing about an inch of darker material.

The original contents of the cist had either completely decayed away or been at some time removed. That the cist had been rifled, perhaps ages ago, seems not impossible from the fact that the cover stones were not in proper position. Careful search was made for any fragments of bone, or pottery, or metal, but nothing of the kind could be detected. In the absence of direct evidence it is impossible to say definitely whether this interment belongs to the bronze or iron age. Reasoning, however, from analogy, we seem entitled to suppose that the former is the more probable. The practice of cairn burial is highly characteristic of the bronze age, and the size of the Mulloch cist corresponds with the typical dimensions of a bronze age cist. In such interments the body was placed in the grave either in a doubled-up position or after having been first cremated. Certain objects are regularly found accompanying the human remains - a small urn with certain distinctive features of shape and ornamentation, cutting weapons of bronze, and other articles of personal use or adornment, such as necklaces, pins, bracelets, and rings, sometimes of gold, never of silver. Though all these, as we have said, were absent in this interment, they have been frequently found in prehistoric graves in the district. For example, on the south side of the Dee, opposite Mulloch, a cist was discovered in a large pile called Cairnmore which contained human remains and a gold chain and pin. Not far off, at Tillycairn, urns containing calcined bones were found many years ago, and, it is said, bronze objects along with them. Near Tarland numerous stone cists have come to light in cairns, some of which contained urns. At Cairn Flumerock, south-east of the Ord, near Dinnet, there is record of other similar interments. (It was doubtless these discoveries from time to time that gave rise to the local belief that the cairns about the Moor of Dinnet and the neighbourhood marked the burial places of Danish chiefs slain in the famous legendary battle of Munandawan). Near Cairn Flumerock many flint arrow-heads were found when the ground was being prepared for the building of Dinnet House.

In addition to the two cairns of which mention has been made, around the base of Mulloch hill may be seen a great number of circular enclosures and round mounds of stones, with embanked roadways wandering through them and leading off both eastward over the ridge of hills stretching to Aboyne, and westward over the flat marshy ground towards Loch Kinnord and the numerous prehistoric stone structures skirting its shores (see pp. 18-23). There are perhaps few districts in Scotland more abundantly supplied with such remains. Almost every acre of uncultivated ground shows traces of them, and frequently they are so clustered together that the whole surface is occupied with them.

The smaller circular mounds vary from 8 to 20 feet in diameter. Only a few have yet been explored, and these have yielded no relics.* Generally the foundations show a circle of stones sunk a little way into the ground, which is scooped out from the enclosed area till the encircling stones appear as if resting on the floor. Where there is any depth of soil this excavation is often as deep as 1 1/2 feet, seldom more. As they now appear, they simply form

[*See note on "The Islands" at the end.]

round heaps which, when examined, disclose structures as described.

The larger class of circles varies from 15 to 24 yards in diameter. The encircling wall is generally from 7 to 12 feet in thickness, but there are often concentric walls of various thickness. In some cases the whole area is occupied by an immense pile of loose stones; in others there are very few stones in the interior. So many have, however, been carted away to build fences and farm-steadings that it would be rash to hazard a conjecture as to what might have been the original quantity.

Along the south base of the hill there are other ancient remains which are distinguished from those we have been describing in being of rectangular, not circular, form. The appearance which they presented about 50 years ago (and in their main features there has not been much alteration) may be given in the words of the Rev. R. M. Miller, Aboyne, a competent observer, who regarded them as defensive structures of some kind or other. "At Knockice are the ruins of three rectangular stone enclosures, all close to and connected with each other. The westmost one, 140 yards by 88, the next larger, and the eastmost about double the size of the other two. All the three have been apparently open on the south side, except in so far as naturally secured by a small rill of water and marshy ground. There are two smaller enclosures, of from 12 to 18 yards diameter, a little out from the north-west corner of the smallest of the three, on steep rising ground and overlooking the whole. The road or diked avenue from Kinnord leads to the westmost of the three and is lost in it. It again appears skirting the other two, except in one place where it is blocked up by the wall of the inclosure, to form which the stones of the two dikes appear in that place to have been removed. It may be noticed that the enclosures had been mere fences of loose stone and turf, without any outside ditch. Three sides of the hill slope as regularly as if they had by art been formed into a glacis, and contain several deep trenches, of no great length, like so many redoubts to check an advancing army; and the whole

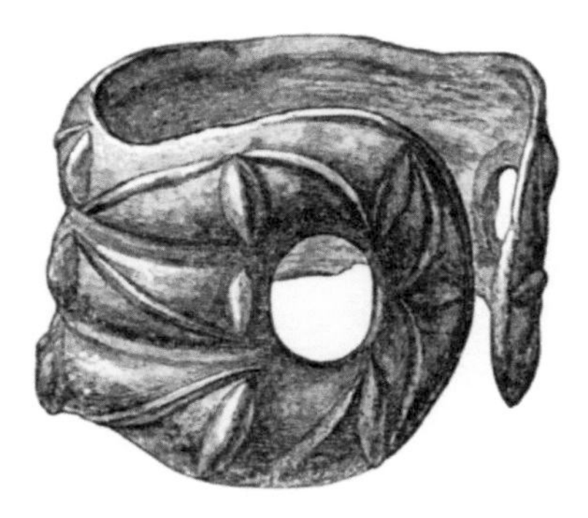

FIG. 12. - BRASS ARMLET (ONE OF THREE) FOUND AT CR0SSFOLD, COULL. FRONT VIEW

ground is covered with cairns, many of them within the enclosures."

Constructions somewhat similar in character occur also in several places on the slopes and heights of Culblean. There is one near Tomgleddy, which exhibits traces of a walled road resembling those at Kinnord and Mulloch. On the north side of the Burn of the Vat, near the old Culblean road, there is another, surmounting which there is a prominent height, covered with heaps of stones, apparently the ruins of a hill-fort.

Whether these rectangular constructions were made by the same people as the circular enclosures may be doubtful. The close association of the two would seem to point to the conclusion that they were. As regards the date of the circular foundations, I have already mentioned that such of them as have been excavated on Mulloch have yielded no relics. Evidence, however, is obtainable in the near neighbourhood which enables us to

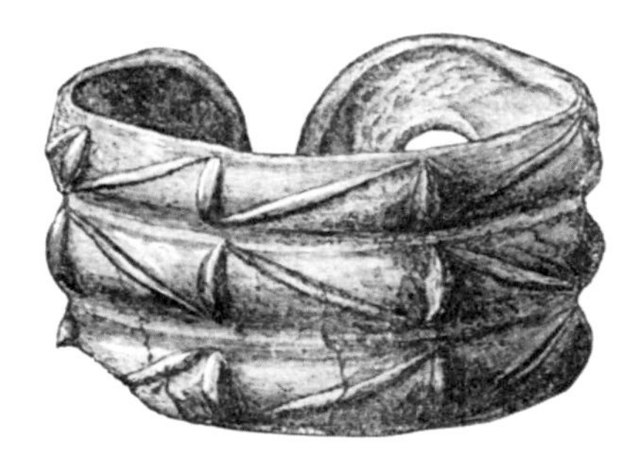

FIG. 13.- BRASS ARMLET FOUND AT CROSSFOLD, COULL. BACK VIEW

fix them as belonging to the Pictish period. Near the church of Logie-Coldstone an underground or Picts' house was found, and close beside it a pavement of considerable extent. Now the interior of these circular enclosures is sometimes paved, and doubtless this was the remains of such a structure. Again, on the farm of Crossfold, Coull, there are two underground houses, near to which there were within living memory two very large and well-defined circular enclosures. When the ground on which they stood was being trenched, three very remarkable brass ornaments, which experts assign to the Early Celtic period, came to light (see pp. 138 and 139).

After an examination of a pretty large number of these stone mounds or cairns and of the circular foundations, I am of opinion that the smaller cairns are the ruins of ancient human dwellings, constructed and occupied in the period immediately preceding the dawn of authentic history. The same type of dwelling may be seen in the western isles. The most likely explanation of the purpose of the circular enclosures seems to be that they were built to protect the inhabitants and their cattle from the depredations of foes and wild beasts. Many of them were doubtless forts with very high walls, but these are easily distinguishable both by the situations they occupy and the huge quantity of stones they contain.

NOTES

BYRON AND MARY ROBERTSON

(See p. 59)

THE question of "Byron's Mary," as far as Mary Robertson of Balletrach is concerned, centres round the verses in *Hours of Idleness* beginning -

> "When I roved a young Highlander o'er the dark heath,
> And climb'd thy steep summit, O Morven of Snow,
> To gaze on the torrent that thunder'd beneath
> Or the mist of the tempest that gather'd below,
> Untutor'd by science, a stranger to fear,
> And rude as the rocks where my infancy grew,
> No feeling, save one, to my bosom was dear;
> Need I say, my sweet Mary, 'twas centr'd in you?"

Who is the Mary referred to?

Till the publication of *Loch Kinnord* (1877) it was generally assumed that Mary Duff, the poet's distant relative, had inspired the verses. Of his early and never-forgotten passion for her there is, of course, no question - we have his own account of it. But Byron's fancy was ever vagrant, and the circumstances of the poem, along with other known facts, point rather to Mary Robertson of Balletrach than to his Aberdeen playmate.

In his ninth year, when attending the Grammar School at Aberdeen, Byron had an attack of illness, and his mother took him in the course of the summer to the country for his health. At that time (1796) the reputation of the Wells of Pannanich, we are told, was drawing "crowds of visitors," who had to find accommodation as they could in the country around about, there being as yet no village of Ballater. Two miles east of Pannanich, on the south side of the Dee, lies the pleasant farm of Balletrach,* of old one of the numerous Farquharson lairdships, and then in the occupancy of James Robertson. The farm is a large one, and at that date the house must have been one of the best of its class, west of Aboyne. It would appear that Robertson was in the way of receiving visitors, and that his farm was known among Aberdeen middle-class people as a suitable place for summer quarters. A stray letter of his is printed in *Scottish Notes and Queries* (1893), of date 1781, written to "Alex. Dingwall, merchant, Aberdeen," and giving particulars of accommodation and charges. Board and lodging cost 10*s*. per week, "shugar, tee, and loaf bread" not included; a riding horse is offered at "5*s*. sterling a week." Doubtless Mrs. Byron had heard of these quarters from Aberdeen acquaintances who had stayed there. It has been suggested that, being a Gordon of Gight and thus standing in some degree of kinship with the Earl of Aboyne, to whom Balletrach belonged, she found her way to this district through this connection. This is unlikely for several reasons, but the point is of no importance. What concerns

*Though Ballater and Balletrach are near neighbours and the names look similar to the eye, they have no etymological connection, the accent in Ballater being on the first syllable, in Balletrach on the second. The Gaelic of the latter is *Bail' leitreach* "(farm) town of the hill slope."

us is that she brought her little son here for a considerable stay in 1796, and again the following year.

At the time of his visits the Robertson household included a large family of boys and two girls. The elder, Jean, was grown up, but her sister Mary was of an age more suitable for playing companion to the Aberdeen stranger. Tradition says that he formed a strong attachment to her.

Mrs. Robertson was the daughter of Captain MacDonald, laird of Rinetan in Glengairn, as stated on p. 59, and the households at Balletrach and Rinetan are known to have kept up a close intercourse. Jean was brought up by her aunts in Glengairn, and Mary was frequently there. Byron appears to have shared in this going and coming, a fact which helps to explain how he should have remembered so much of the Highlands, though only a child at the time. The various allusions in his works and letters prove how strongly the scenes and incidents of his Deeside holidays had impressed themselves on his mind. His Glengairn visits can also be traced in his note to *Childe Harold*, canto II, on the Albanians. He draws a detailed comparison between them and the Highlanders of Scotland, and is struck among other resemblances by the similarity of the sound of their language to the Celtic. Now he would have heard no Gaelic at Balletrach, but in Glengairn it was the current speech at the time.

When *Hours of Idleness* appeared and Byron's reputation penetrated to his old haunts on Deeside, the people of the district were quick to recognise in his boyish companion the "Mary" of the verses. The language also and whole setting of the poem accord most naturally with this identification.

Mr. Michie's view is confirmed independently, as he was able to point out (*Rec. of Invercauld*, p. 392), in the Memoir of Stewart Clark (a Deeside man), where the author records that a William Clark, who lived near Pannanich "was also a great favourite with the boy Byron .... He used to positively declare that the Mary mentioned in Byron's poems called 'Hours of Idleness' was not Mary Duff, as commonly supposed, but a Mary Robertson, who lived in a place called Garnshill [Gairnshiel - mistake for Rinetan, which is not far off] near the foot of Morven. The Robertsons were of good family, and Byron used often to go to Garnshill to fish in the Gairn and often talked of his lady love, being a very precocious boy."

As against this identification, it has been pointed out that according to the date on her tombstone Mary Robertson was six years older than the poet. Thus in the summer when he was nine, she would have been fifteen, a disparity that it is hard to reconcile with a childish attachment between them. The apparent difficulty, however, arises from a curious blunder, which was first pointed out to the present writer by Mr. Charles Brown, formerly of Coldstone and an old pupil of Michie's, who has taken much interest in this new edition of *L. Kinnord* and has lent valuable assistance on various points. Mary Robertson's age, 85, as given on the tombstone, is a mistake. However the blunder may have arisen (possibly it came about from her having died a childless widow, with no near relatives at hand to keep the date right), Mr. Brown has discovered from the parochial registers of Glenmuick that she was born in December 1785, and was thus not six years older than Byron, but only two years, one month. Mr. Brown has also made enquiries of a cousin of hers, who knew her well in later life, but the only details of interest which he learned were that Mary was of about medium height, perhaps rather under it, and, without being a beauty, was good-looking; that her hair was fair, as in the poem - "I think on the long flowing ringlets of gold"; and that she often spoke of Byron, but in a general way. The only particular her cousin could call to mind was that she frequently referred to him as having been a "very delicate boy."

THE SCULPTURED STONES

UPPER DEESIDE, and in particular the district in which Loch Kinnord is situated, is remarkably rich in that class of archaeological remains commonly known as Sculptured Stones. In the churchyard of Tullich alone there are preserved no fewer than six examples, while in many counties of Scotland there is not so much as a single specimen, at least of the older type of stone. The historical interest attaching to these monuments is very great, and, in respect of one of their features, they have the additional attraction of offering a problem - presently to be referred to - which it has as yet baffled archaeological science to solve.

Some account is given of three of the Tullich Stones at pp. 118-123, and of the Kinnord specimen at p. 31. In view, however, of the fact that they will be more fully understood when studied along with others of the same nature, it seems desirable to give a complete list of all the early monuments of this class which have been found in the district, and to indicate briefly the results of the latest investigations regarding their history and significance.

There are on Upper Deeside thirteen incised or sculptured slabs which can be referred to a date earlier than the 12th or 13th century. This is the inferior limit of time, the superior limit being for some of the stones very much earlier. It is generally supposed that most, if not all of them, served the purpose of sepulchral monuments.

I. - TULLICH (plate VIII and fig. 9, p. 118). This belongs to the class known as "symbol" stones (see below), and from a comparison with others bearing the same symbols it is evident that it has been mutilated at both sides. The photograph fails to give a very clear view of the incised figures, but the outline drawing, which is from a rubbing reduced by photography, shows their form with accuracy.

FIG. 14. - THE TOMACHAR STONE (SEE PLATE OPPOSITE) FROM A RUBBING.

II. - TOMACHAR. When attention was first called to this stone (plate IX and fig. 14,) it was built into a wall at

Pl.IX.

THE TOMACHAR STONE

the farm of Mill of Newton in the parish of Logie-Coldstone. It was known, however, that it had originally stood on the top of a knoll near by, called Tomachar (accent on the last syllable; Gael. *Tom a' chathair*, moss-hillock). It now stands within the grounds of Tillypronie House, where it was removed by the late Sir John F. Clark. (Sir John recognised that the proper place for these historic monuments is their original site, but he excused himself by the fact that the stone had already been moved, and in its second position ran great risk of damage. During his life-time it was readily accessible to anyone who wished to examine it). The stone is 3 feet 4 inches high, 1 foot 8 inches wide, 1 foot 2 inches thick, and stands on a modern base. It has suffered damage at some time or other, either by the weather or other agencies, but two symbolic figures yet remain.

FIG. 15. - THE CORRACHREE STONE

III. - CORRACHREE (in Logie-Coldstone). This stone stands in a field near Logiemar House. It is 5 feet high, 4 feet wide, and 2 feet thick, but much mutilated. One complete symbol remains and fragments of other two (see fig. 15).

IV. - CRAIGMYLE. This striking monolith, the largest of all our examples, is situated on the summit of a considerable elevation near the mansion-house of Craigmyle, Torphins. It was first described by Mr. Michie in *Scottish Notes and Queries,* 1897, his attention having been called to it by Mr. John Ogg, Aberdeen, who remembered noticing with curiosity the incised figures on the great stone when a boy. Its dimensions are - height 7 feet 6 inches, width 4 feet 6 inches, thickness 1 foot 3 inches to 2 feet. In our illustration (plate x), the outlines of the two symbols appear to be white. Mr. Williams, The Schoolhouse, Torphins, who took the photograph for the illustration, which originally appeared in *S. N & Q*, explains that though the incised figures are quite clear to the eye on the stone, they would be difficult to show in a photograph in their natural state, and that he therefore adopted the plan of going carefully over the outlines with chalk before photographing.

V. - FORMASTON. This is sometimes known as the Aboyne stone from its present position at Aboyne Castle, but it is named more properly from the spot where it was originally found, viz., within the churchyard at the Kirk of Formaston, a mile or two east of the village of Aboyne. Evidently only a fragment of the original monument remains (plate IV, p. 50). The intertwined ornamentation in relief is part of the shaft of a cross, as may be seen by comparison with similar slabs. To the right of the shaft is "the mirror symbol," and nearer the edge are two lines of

Pl X.

THE CRAIGMYLE STONE

Ogham writing (see below). The slab is 30 inches by 18 inches in its present state. (The other stone in the illustration, which is lying in front of the slab, has no connection with it. We have been unable to ascertain what it is or how it came there).

VI. - MIGVIE. In the churchyard stands a large pillar stone, 6 feet 2 inches high, 2 feet 5 inches wide at the bottom, of a roughly rectangular shape (plate v, p. 64). On the front there are 5 different sculpturings, (1) a cross formed of interlaced work, (2) at the left of the top arm a "symbol" design, (3) at the right of the top arm another symbol, (4) at the left of the shaft a pair of shears, (5) at the right of the shaft a man on horseback. On the back is another figure of a horse and rider. These last two, it should be mentioned, have been deliberately tampered with. Andrew Jervise, the antiquary, who was in the district about the time of the discovery of the stone, writes: "On my second visit I was shocked to find that some goth had re-chiselled and bevelled away the originally simple, yet bold and characteristic outlines of the equestrian figures."

The Migvie monolith came to light among the foundation stones of the old church. It was dug out of a burial aisle in 1861, its own interment there being assignable, we may suppose, to post-Reformation times. Michie was of opinion that this monument is the same as a stone frequently mentioned in very early charters of the Earls of Mar, who at that time possessed the lands in this neighbourhood. From these writs it appears that the Lords Superior were accustomed to hold their courts for the district at the Stone of Migvie,"*apud lapidem de Migveth*".

Their castle was situated within a few hundred yards of the church, and it seems quite likely that in this elaborately sculptured pillar we have the stone at which the Earls and their vassals met, and which was already a remarkable and venerable object about the 12th and 13th centuries.

VII. - KINNORD (plate III, p. 31). Now at Aboyne Castle, its original position having been, as stated on p. 31, on the north shore of Loch Kinnord near the site where tradition says once stood a chapel. The dimensions are height, 6 feet 3 inches; width, 3 feet 1 inch; thickness, 1 foot. There are no "symbols" in this case, but an elaborately sculptured cross occupies nearly the whole surface of the slab, which has been roughly shaped. In the photograph the curious and intricate ramifications of the interlacing can be seen. There are five different patterns in the whole figure, and a comparison with the plait-work on Nos. IV and V (pp. 50 and 64) will show with what fertility these early artists varied their designs.

VIII. - COLDSTONE (fig. 10, p. 121). In the churchyard there is one stone which from its small size may easily escape notice. It is placed as the headstone of a grave, and measures 22 by 11 inches. On the face an oval has been sunk, and within the oval a Celtic cross sculptured in relief. The whole design is simple and unpretentious, but from the delicacy and balance of the parts the effect is highly artistic. Sir Arthur Mitchell, who described it in the *Proceedings of the Society of Antiquaries*, vol. x, called attention to the "great character" of this little monument.

IX-XIII. - TULLICH. Within the same enclosure as No. I there are five slabs with incised Celtic crosses, which from their design can be ascribed to a period earlier than the 12th century or thereabout (plate VIII, p. 118). Two of them are marked B and C on the plate; the other three are smaller.

Such being the group of early monuments still surviving in our district, their origin, history, and meaning can only be settled by comparing them with objects of the same nature found in other parts of Scotland or elsewhere. Till recently this would have been a work of considerable difficulty. A full list would have been unobtainable, and such monuments as had been noted and described would have had to be hunted for in whatever publication they chanced to be recorded. Many were imperfectly described and figured, many unnoted altogether. Thanks, however, to the magnificent work issued in 1903 under the auspices of the Society of Antiquaries of Scotland by J. Romilly Allen and Dr. Joseph Anderson - the *Early Christian Monuments of Scotland* - the enquirer has now before him in one volume a complete list, illustrated, described, and classified, with an analysis of their symbolism and ornamentation.

Following the guidance of these authors, we find that the ancient Scottish stone monuments (of which there are over 500 examples similar in character to those described above), once they can be brought together under one review, are seen to fall naturally into three classes.

A. - *Monuments with incised symbols only*. The stones on which the designs are cut are either natural pillars which have received no shaping, or rude slabs which have received very little.

B. - *Monuments with symbols and Celtic ornament carved in relief*. In this class the stone has been more carefully prepared, being generally shaped into a rectangular form and the surface dressed.

C. - *Monuments with Celtic ornament in relief.* The symbols have now disappeared, and the monuments have greater variety of form. We have still upright cross slabs, but also free-standing crosses, recumbent slabs, and other varieties. The artistic advance, which shows itself in class B, is continued. The centuries which saw the full development of this monumental sculpture are also those in which Celtic art reached its culmination in other fields.

A little consideration will show that the order in which these classes are enumerated is also their order in time. Class B is the connecting link between the other two, in respect that on the one hand it contains symbols which class A possesses but class C wants, while on the other it contains decorative ornament which C possesses but A wants. Other considerations, such as the continuous development from less to more ornate, point to the same conclusion. Such being the relative order, it is possible to go a step further and fix an approximately precise date for each class. For the complete argument the reader must be referred to Romilly Allen and Anderson's work and elsewhere. The conclusions that are now generally accepted are, that monuments of class A are to be dated as anterior to 600 or 700 A.D., those of class B as not later than 800 or 900, and those of class C as not later than 1100 or 1200. There may of course have been overlapping at the times of transition, and the dates may vary within limits in different parts of the country, but the above chronology may be taken as well ascertained.

Turning now to the monuments of western Deeside, and examining them in the light of this classification, we find that of *stones with incised symbols only* (class A) there are four examples, the Tullich, Tomachar, Corrachree, and Craigmyle stones (Nos. I-IV above).

At a first glance, these figures are seen to be of an unusual character; they look mysterious, most of them even bizarre. The first impulse is naturally to try to find in the figures pictorial representations of known objects, and while this is in a measure successful with some of them, with others it is plainly impossible. On the Tullich stone, for, instance, the design at the foot is not unlike a hand-mirror (fig. 9, p. 118), but the one at the top suggests a geometrical diagram or pattern. Similarly, the two figures on the Tomachar example (fig. 14, p. 150) are geometrical, while on the Craigmyle monolith (p. 152), though there is no mistaking the presence of a serpent, that it is not the mere picture of a serpent is at once suggested by the geometrical design immediately above it. The sculpturing therefore of these and similar monuments is universally regarded as symbolic, but what ideas the emblems called up in the minds of those who understood them is at present a mere matter of conjecture, hardly even of that. Up to date there have been noted in all 192 symbol-bearing stones (124 of class A and 68 of class B), and the number of different symbols employed is 46.* Some of them are of much more frequent occurrence than others, and all of them are found in groups or combinations rather than singly. They may be divided into three classes - (1) geometrical figures, (2) figures of objects of known use, (3) figures of beasts, birds, etc.

* The symbols have also been noted, on the walls of caves, and on a few obiects of metal, such as chains, and of bone.

The fact that the same figures occur all over the area where the monuments are found proves that their function was not pictorial but symbolic or emblematic. Thus, it is conceivable that the sculptor of the Craigmyle stone, for example, might have incised a picture of a serpent as an exercise of his artistic powers, but when the same serpent makes its appearance in similar circumstances in places as far apart as Ross and Perth, it is clear that we have to do with some recognised convention. The pattern of any given symbol is fixed, re-appearing in practically identical form in all its occurrences.

Of the whole forty-six there are four which from their numerical preponderance may be regarded as the principal symbols.

(a) The symbol called the crescent and V-shaped rod occurs fifty-nine times (fig. 16). It is the lower of the two figures on the Tomachar stone (p. 150).

FIGS. 16 - 17

(b) The double disc and Z-shaped rod occurs forty-nine times (fig. 17). It may be seen at the top of the Tullich stone (p. 118).

(c) The mirror and comb symbol (fig. 18). This is

wanting in our Deeside examples, but the mirror without the comb occurs at Tullich and also on the Formaston stone (p. 50). A fact has been noticed about this symbol which can hardly be accidental. Wherever it occurs on monuments of class A in combination with other symbols, it stands at the foot, as at Tullich. Also it has been remarked that combinations of two principal symbols are found repeated on other monuments, but with the addition of the mirror or mirror and comb. Dr. Anderson supposes the meaning of this to be that "what is told by the first two symbols was told of males and females, and that certain groups of symbols were made applicable to females by the addition of the mirror and comb as a female determinative." It occurs forty-four times.

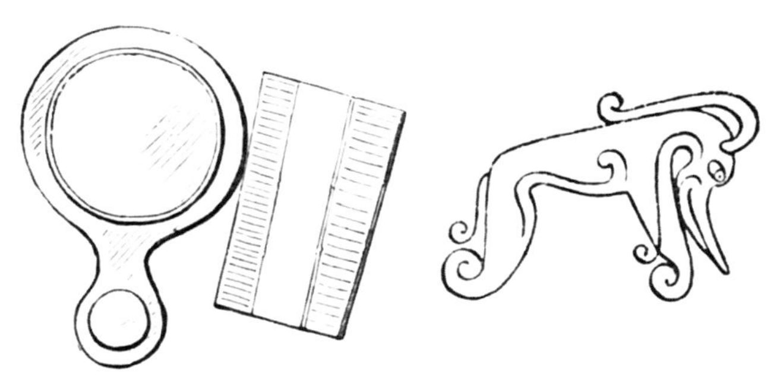

FIGS. 18 - 19

(d) A symbol which may be described as a conventional representation of a beast with long jaws, crest, and scroll-feet, sometimes, but not very happily, called the "elephant" symbol (fig. 19). There are thirty-three examples recorded in all, one of which is at

Tullich - the middle figure on the slab (p. 118).

Besides these four widely distributed symbols, the stones in our district contain others. The upper of the two on the Tomachar stone (p. 150) is known as the 2-legged rectangle with Z-shaped rod. (The same Z rod appears in the double disc above). It seems to be the upper figure on the Craigmyle stone (p. 152), though the exact outline is doubtful owing to weathering. There are only nine examples recorded in all, and as seven of them occur on stones of class A, it must be regarded as one of the primitive symbols. It was probably falling into disuse by the time that monuments of class B were devised.

The serpent symbol, seen on the Craigmyle stone, has been noted ten times elsewhere, and there are also ten examples of it accompanied by the same Z-shaped rod which we have seen twice above (fig. 20).

FIG. 20

The Corrachree symbols (p. 151) are so much defaced that two of them cannot be made out. The top one is a circular disc with a triskele. Discs in various forms, single, double, and even triple, are well represented on the monuments.

Coming now to stones of class B, those containing *Symbols and Celtic ornament carved in relief* (see above,

P. I55), we have two examples in our district, Nos. V and VI, p. 152, 153.

As mentioned above, the Migvie monolith (p. 64) has three symbols. The double disc and Z-shaped rod we have already seen at Tullich, but the other two are unique. The horse-shoe symbol (on the right of the upper arm of the cross) is found eleven times, in every case on monuments of the primitive class, but never with the V-shaped rod as here. The object also on the left of the shaft, which looks like a pair of shears, has been noted nowhere else.

Enough remains of the Formaston slab (p. 50) to show that it belongs to class B. The mirror symbol without the comb shows very clearly on the dressed surface.

Class C, *monuments with Celtic ornament carved in relief* and without symbols, is represented by only one stone in our district, the cross slab found at Kinnord (p. 31), though elsewhere this group is by far the most numerous.

Nos. VIII and IX-XIII of the list given on pp. 150-154 do not fall into any of the three great divisions. The symbols and the interlaced ornament are both wanting. In No. VIII (p. 121) the cross is carved in relief, and in the other five (plate VIII, p.118) the crosses are incised. The Logie-Coldstone cross is of very early type, as are most of the Tullich ones, except possibly the stone marked C on plate VIII and mentioned at p. 120.

In the absence of all knowledge of what the symbols mean, the question of whether they belong to pre-Christian or Christian times has given rise to considerable discussion. Some archaeologists, founding upon the total dissimilarity of these figures to any other known Christian symbols, have had no difficulty in accepting them as the products of

Pagan religion and art. They point out that there is nothing about the most primitive of the symbol-incised monuments to suggest a Christian origin, not even their situation, which is often, as in the case of the Tomachar and Craigmyle examples, a spot unconnected with any ecclesiastical associations. This view, however, is hardly convincing; it fails to take into account some of the facts of the problem. Though it is true that the oldest symbol stones contain nothing which *we* can recognise as Christian, it is evident that the sculptors of the crosses found nothing inconsistent with Christianity in the so-called Pagan emblems, for on all those monuments which we have discussed as class B, they are freely associated with the cross. On the Pagan theory, the only way of accounting for this is to suppose that this elaborate system of symbolism was taken over into the new religion and utilised for its purposes. This seems a somewhat precarious hypothesis, more especially as it would be difficult to parallel such a transference in any other field where Christianity supplanted Paganism. Besides, though it is true that some of the monuments belong to non-ecclesiastical sites, it is possible that these sites may once have had Christian buildings which have now disappeared and been forgotten; and in any case, it cannot be denied that many of the stones have been found in intimate association with Christian churches, as for instance at Tullich. It is hard to believe that the Christian missionaries would not only have tolerated these monuments but preserved them at their new foundations, if the figures which they bore were the insignia, so to say, of the cult which they were labouring to destroy. The balance of opinion, therefore, is in favour of the conclusion that if the symbols have a religious significance, as apparently they must have, they are Christian.

But while the symbols have so far guarded the secret of their significance, their lineage is less difficult to read. If we disregard their meaning and attend only to their appearance and characteristic forms, we observe that they possess certain features in which they resemble the Celtic art-work of the Pagan period. Abundant remains of this art-work, especially in objects of metal, are available for purposes of comparison, and though the decoration of the symbols is meagre there is enough to show that it belongs to the same school. We may conclude, therefore, that the primitive symbol-monuments lie, if not within, then very close to the Pagan period.

DISTRIBUTION OF THE SCULPTURED STONES. - A study of the monuments from the point of view of their geographical distribution brings some new facts into light. As stated before, there are over 500 remaining in Scotland to-day, all of which must be reckoned older than the 12th or 13th century. (During those centuries the Celtic church was transformed by the invasion of English, Norman and foreign ecclesiastics, and its native art disappeared under these alien influences. The grave-slabs and similar monuments henceforth lose their native peculiarities, and are fashioned in the style common to Western Europe).

If we divide Scotland into districts we find that the monuments are distributed as follows:- in the section south of the Forth there are 108 examples; in the section north of the Forth but west of the mountain range formerly known as Drumalban, i.e. roughly, the modern Argyll, there are 27;

in the remaining section, north of the Forth and east of Drumalban, there are 373. The comparative paucity in the first two districts is at once apparent, and in the case of the second this is specially striking, because in it is included Iona, which is commonly regarded as the centre from which the Celtic or "Iona" cross originated.

If now we exclude from consideration the monuments of class C, and confine ourselves to those bearing the symbols either alone or in conjunction with the cross, there are 192 in all. With one solitary exception found south of the Forth, the whole of these belong to northern Scotland, east of Drumalban. Argyll and the neighbourhood yield not a single specimen.

And lastly, taking into account the primitive stones, with symbols only, we have 124 examples. Of these 41 have been found in Aberdeen, 15 in Sutherland, 14 in Inverness, 12 in Elgin, 7 in Forfar, 6 in Ross, 6 in Banff, 6 in Kincardine, 5 in Perth, 3 in Shetland, 3 in Caithness, 2 in Orkney, 2 in the Hebrides, 1 in Fife, 1 in Midlothian. The rest of Scotland is blank.

Now from historical sources we know that in the 5th and succeeding centuries, after the withdrawal of the Romans from Britain, what is now Scotland was divided politically into four parts. North of the Forth and east of Drumalban were the kingdoms of the Northern and Southern Picts, the dividing line being the Grampian range; west of Drumalban (roughly the modern Argyll), the kingdom of the Dalriadic Scots; in the south-west the Britons of Strathclyde; and in the south-east, part of the Anglian kingdom of Bernicia. Comparing the range of the symbol stones with these political divisions, we see that it coincides exactly with ancient Pictavia, and the conclusion is irresistible that this symbolism originated and was developed there. As nothing resembling these monuments has ever been observed in any other area, they can rightly be regarded as indigenous. Similarly with the more elaborate stones of class B, which are also confined to the same district, though some of their decorative features can be paralleled in Irish MS. work, their most distinctive and attractive characteristics are unborrowed and must be credited to the invention and taste of the men who fashioned them - a conclusion that can hardly fail to suggest some reflections on the commonly received "barbarism" of the Picts and Scots.*

ABERDEENSHIRE AND THE SYMBOLS. - The comparative distribution of the primitive symbol stones, as given

*The neglect with which these remarkable monuments have been treated is a signal proof of the dominance of the classical tradition among us. Had they been Greek or Roman, instead of Celtic, it is easy to conceive the care with which even the fragments would have been gathered up, and the enthusiasm with which scholars would have flung themselves on their elucidation. As it is, little is done to preserve them from destruction, and except for a few specialists or antiquaries they are for the most part unheeded. And yet, if only on the score of antiquity, their credentials are highly respectable and might have attracted more attention. To put it chronologically, the ascertained fact that our own Northern Scotland is rich in remains, the oldest of which are practically contemporary with Justinian and Sancta Sophia, is sufficiently striking. But intrinsically too, the whole field of Celtic archaeology and art is, in the opinion of competent authorities, well worthy of wider study. Dr. Joseph Anderson, of the National Museum, than whom there is no one better qualified to speak, has put on record his judgment that if, along with the monumental sculpturing, the Celtic metal work and MSS. of the same school be taken into account, "the whole series, considering the work and time, presents a manifestation of artistic culture altogether unparalleled in Europe."

above, suggests a further remark or two; Aberdeenshire possesses no fewer than 42 out of the total 124. What is the significance of this preponderance?

It is of course true that the monuments which survive to-day are probably only a remnant of those that originally existed, and that the relative frequency as observed to-day may not correspond with that of ancient times. But if this is so, then it can only be because some agency, tending to preserve or destroy the original monuments, has been at work more powerfully in some districts than in others. Nothing, however, is known of any such cause, and the most natural explanation of the difference in distribution to-day seems to be that the difference always existed. On this assumption, therefore, the fabrication of these symbol stones attained a wider prevalence in Aberdeenshire than in any other part of Scotland. This county may be regarded as the focus where the system of symbolism originated, and from which it spread to surrounding parts. We are even tempted to go further and point to the neighbourhood of Kintore and Inverurie as the birth-place of the symbols, to judge from the striking richness of that locality in symbol-stones.*

The other counties where these remains are found in any abundance are all north of the Grampians. In fact, there are only twelve specimens to the south. It is thus clear that the symbols both originated and found most favour among the Northern Picts.

The conclusion thus reached regarding Aberdeenshire is confirmed by an analysis of the occurrence of the symbols separately. Of the whole forty-six a greater

* *Early Christian Monuments of Scotland*, Pt. II., p. 13.

number are represented in this county than anywhere else, and the commoner ones are found in larger numbers.

From the range of these monuments too, we have a means of forming some notion of the state of population and civilisation in any given district in Pictish times. Romilly Allen points out that in Scotland generally "the monuments, are in no instance found in the barren mountainous districts, which are often so prolific in remains of an earlier period, but in the fertile lands near the coast or in the great river valleys. The western or inland parts of Sutherland, Ross, and Inverness are entirely destitute of sculptured stones." In the four north eastern counties, however, they occur much further inland, as in the case of the stones in our district. We are thus entitled to infer that in Pictish times western Deeside was well peopled, and that its civilisation and culture had reached the level of the period. No monuments have been found west of Tullich, but in the absence of a thorough examination of the numerous ecclesiastical sites in Crathie and Braemar, it is too soon to say that none exist.

As the primitive symbol stones fell out of fashion and the new style of monument with cross and symbols was developed, the lead passed from Aberdeenshire. Of the 68 examples that remain, 32 belong to Forfar, and 16 to Perth. In all Northern Pictland there are only 17, our two examples at Migvie and Formaston being of the number. The provenance of this class of monument is thus essentially Pictavia of the South.

When the third style - the non-symbol stone - appears, its range is no longer, as in the case of the other two, confined to the Northern and Southern Picts, but extends over Scotland. The same poverty of examples, however, continues in Aberdeenshire, only intensified. The Kinnord stone and one at Fyvie are the solitary representatives of this, the most widely spread, type. It is difficult to assign a very satisfactory explanation for this, more especially as some of the other northern counties, such as Ross and Elgin, make a much better show. In a general way the reason may be that the centuries to which monuments of this type belong saw the completion of important political changes, by which under Kenneth MacAlpin and his successors the various kingdoms were consolidated into the one kingdom of Alban or Scotland, and the centre of gravity, politically and ecclesiastically, established to the south of the Grampians. At any rate it is in that region that the development of these beautifully designed and decorated stones reaches its maximum.

THE FORMASTON OGHAM. - It will probably have been remarked that none of the Deeside stones which have been discussed seem to bear anything of the nature of letters or inscriptions. There is, however, one exception - the Formaston (Aboyne) cross-slab. Between the cross shaft and the right-hand edge (plate IV, p. 50) there can be clearly seen two rows of Ogham lettering, one on the smooth surface, the other on the marginal beading.

Inscriptions in this alphabet are extant in Ireland, in Wales and the adjoining parts of England, and in Scotland. It is entirely confined to the Celtic area, and bears no resemblance to any other known European alphabetic system. It was not, however, the only alphabet used by the early Celts; many of the monuments in Wales bear bi-lingual inscriptions, the same epigraph being incised in

Roman letters and in Oghams. The Ogham key can thus be deduced from these bi-linguals. But the use of this alphabet was not confined to monuments in stone; it occurs in early Irish MSS, and several of them give a transliteration from Ogham into ordinary Irish script. The key, as given in the Book of Ballimote, is as follows-

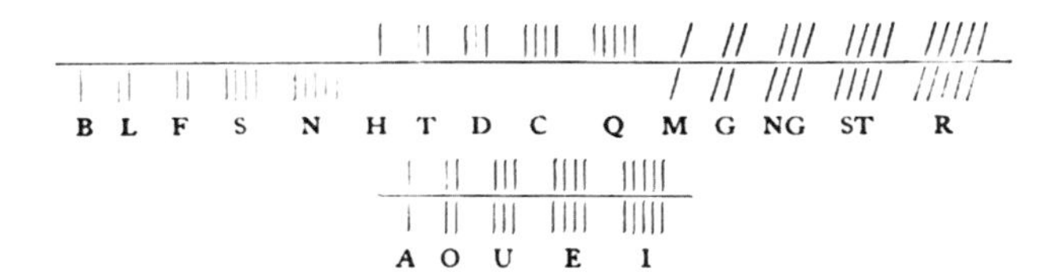

As compared with the inscriptions in Wales and Ireland little success has attended the interpretation of the Scottish Oghams. Till some sort of unanimity is apparent among the various readings that have been proposed, it is impossible to believe that they have been correctly deciphered. As it is, the number of readings offered is just about equal to the number of experts who have examined them. There are several reasons for this uncertainty. In many cases the stones are worn and defaced, and the inscriptions fragmentary and barely legible. Then again, as the Ogham alphabet is easily susceptible of various modifications, it is quite likely that in the Scottish examples some of the characters may have values peculiar to this area; and lastly, as the forms of the early Celtic in which they are written are problematical, the readings that may be proposed cannot be directly tested. In spite of all difficulties, however, the correct decipherment of the Scottish Oghams is one of the most important and fascinating problems for modern Celtic scholarship.

Seventeen or eighteen inscriptions in this alphabet are known up to date, and all of them but one occur in the same districts as the symbol-bearing stones discussed above. They are by far the oldest specimens of the Celtic language of Scotland in existence, their dates lying probably between 600 and 1000 A.D.

To return to our inscription. Though in point of preservation and legibility it is one of the best, none of the readings can be said to have attained general acceptance, more especially as regards the second line. There is more consensus of opinion regarding the first, which may provisionally be held to run (reading from the bottom to the top) MAQQOI TALLUORRH, the meaning being "the son," or, if the first word is in the genitive case, (the grave) "of the son of Talluorrh." Whether this rendering be ultimately confirmed or not, it can meantime be said to make sense, for Talorg is a personal name that has a real existence. It occurs in the lists of Pictish kings, and there was also a Pictish saint of the same name in its diminutive form, Talorgan, which survives in Kiltarlity (Ross-shire), "church of Talorgan." (Watson, P.N. of, *Ross and Crom.*, p. 33). He was also the patron saint of the Church of Fordyce where there is, or was, a well called after him.

As to the meaning and etymology of *Talorg*, they seem to be well ascertained: the authorities derive from tal, 'brow,' and the root arg, org, 'white,' the same as is seen in Lat. argentum. Talorg, therefore, is a descriptive proper name, 'White brow.' The same elements occur in the Gaulish Argiotalus (with the same meaning), and one of them in Dubnotalus, 'Deep brow.'

THE ISLANDS, ETC.

FROM Mr. Michie's notes and memoranda for the new edition of *Loch Kinnord* it appears that, after reading Dr. Robert Munro's *Ancient Scottish Lake-dwellings*, he proposed to make some additions to his account of the Crannog (see pp. 93-6). At the time of his death, however, this part of the book, in which he meant to incorporate the results of recent discoveries, was still unwritten. In the present note some attempt is made to supply the deficiency on the lines indicated by the author.

Though attention had long ago been called to the existence of artificial islands or crannogs on many of our lochs, exact information regarding them was for the most part wanting, till their examination was systematically taken up in the south-west of Scotland under the auspices of the Ayrshire and Wigtownshire Archaeological Association and especially by Dr. Munro, who, in the above-mentioned work and afterwards in his *Lake-dwellings of Europe*, made the first scientific study of the whole subject. The important discoveries, which resulted from the examination of these crannogs in the south-west, were due partly to the fact that the explorations were made under the guidance of skilled archaeologists, and partly to the advantageous condition of the crannogs themselves. In most cases, owing to the filling up or drainage of the lochs, the islands practically formed part of the dry land, and hence could be thoroughly dissected and their structure laid bare down to the original lake-floor on which they rested. Before, however, referring to the mechanical principles, as there revealed, upon which the builders of artificial islands proceeded, something may be said of the archaeological relics which were brought to light.

On penetrating below the surface of the mounds - for this was the general appearance that the former islands now presented - the explorers at once met with abundant evidence of ancient human occupation. Fireplaces of clay and stones were found at various levels, with ashes, bones, and domestic *debris* of miscellaneous character. Though the bones of wild animals were present, they were greatly outnumbered by those of the domestic species - the ox, sheep, and pig - and from the large number of querns it is evident that the inhabitants depended for their subsistence rather on agriculture and cattle-rearing than on the chase. The objects of human manufacture were very numerous, and the variety of their material and of the purposes for which they were fashioned, as well as the excellence of the workmanship, indicate a comparatively advanced state of civilisation. Besides the querns just mentioned, other objects of stone were hammers, whetstones, polishers, whorls, polished discs, flint scrapers, jet rings and ornaments. Bronze was largely represented, not so much by implements and weapons as by articles of luxury and personal adornment, such as brooches (some of them of handsome design), pins, rings, and basins. Bone needles, pins, and combs were found pretty frequently. The complete list of the relics made of iron is too extensive to be quoted here, but it may be mentioned that knives, chisels, nails, spear-heads, daggers, saws, shears and pickaxes were all represented; the designer of the bridle-bit of iron and bronze, found in a refuse heap, was not content with producing merely an object of utility, but aimed at a little work of art. The remains of a few articles of leather, one of them a shoe with stamped ornamentation, were recovered; vitreous beads were fairly common; and some articles of wood, apparently for domestic purposes, were recognised.

Certain of the relics are specially significant as throwing light on the date of the crannogs. The Dowalton lake-dwelling yielded a bronze saucepan of Roman manufacture, with the name of the maker stamped on the handle. Almost all of them contained fragments of Samian ware, which is regarded as a certain sign of contact with Roman civilisation. The inference, therefore, is plain that these lake-dwellings had been in occupancy at least up to, and probably later than, Roman times, but how long before it is impossible to say. The general character of the relics indicates clearly the Iron Age; their ornamentation and art forms are equally clearly Early Celtic.

Besides the great collection of archaeological material from these crannogs, the most important result of Dr. Munro's painstaking researches was that for the first time a clear idea was obtained of the structural forms of the islands. Whether all the Scottish lake-dwellings are constructed in the same manner is a matter for further enquiry, but the indications at present are that the main principles of this curious type of stronghold are identical over the whole area. Crannogs are of three kinds - those made of wood entirely, those made of a combination of wood and stones, those made of stones alone. The last being much the least common, our remarks will be confined to the first two.

The appearance of one of these islands, rising with sloping sides from the loch floor in a depth of perhaps ten feet or more of water, suggests at first sight that it must have been built up from the bottom; the rows of piles too would seem to point to the same conclusion. This, however, was not the plan adopted: wherever it has been possible to make a thorough examination of a crannog it becomes apparent that the builders had proceeded on exactly the reverse principle. The first step was to form on the surface of the loch a raft of logs, often resting upon heather or brushwood if the bottom was muddy. Upon this raft layers of stones and logs were deposited, the logs being pinned together and beams being run at intervals from the exterior margin towards the interior and sometimes across the whole diameter of the island. The mass was thus securely bound together. At the same time piles were inserted into prepared holes, giving it additional stability and preventing it from spreading out and collapsing. As the materials were gradually built up, the structure naturally sank, till finally it rested on the bottom, and the crannog was formed. Afterwards the sides were often further strengthened by the addition of stones and beams.

Some of the smaller crannogs are made of wood entirely, but in most cases, as for example the Prison Island on Kinnord, stones are freely employed. In fact, very often the presence of wooden beams can only be detected by digging into the interior; to all appearance the island looks like a natural cairn.

The mechanical skill exhibited in the construction of large artificial islands in this unexpected manner, islands, it should be noted, which have resisted the destructive agencies of two thousand years at least, must have been of a high order. Dr. Munro's minute researches on their structural features impressed this deeply on his mind. As he says, an engineer of the present day might be puzzled if confronted with the problem which the early crannog builders successfully solved, and modern science would fail to produce better results under the given conditions.

Unlike the Prison Island, its bigger neighbour has generally been regarded as entirely natural. Dr. John Stuart, F.S.A. Scot., who examined it in 1855, thought it might be partly artificial; he was struck by the existence of submerged beams of black oak, and, as we shall see presently, the fact was well worthy of consideration. Mr. Wattie of Bellastraid, who described the loch and islands in a paper to the Society of Antiquaries about the same date, when Scottish "crannogology" was beginning to attract attention, could see no signs of artificiality, and Mr. Michie agreed with him (p. 93), though at the same time he mentions the fact that the stones on the island beach are considerably larger than those on the adjacent land shore. In general appearance the island certainly looks natural enough; it is covered with a carpet of green grass; there are no traces of piling to be seen either above or below water; and, most of all, the great size of the island - about 100 yards in length by 70 in breadth - seems to negative the idea of its having been put together by human agency. Nevertheless, the possibility of its being really a crannog cannot be summarily dismissed. The ascertained fact that the great majority of islands in our lochs are not natural, raises a presumption that the Castle Island may belong to the same class. The recent investigations carried on by the Rev. Odo Blundell, O.S.B., show that there are some large islands in the north whose general appearance of being natural is misleading. One of these is on Loch Bruiach near Beauly. It is distant about 100 yards from the nearest shore, and is 64 yards long by 34 yards broad, being thus only about half the size of the Castle Island, but still a remarkable structure if it was artificially put together in primitive times in the manner described above. That this must have been the case, Mr. Blundell was able to prove very effectively. He had the use of a diving apparatus, and once below water he observed beams of wood running through the stones. Similarly with the island called Cairn Dubh in the Beauly Firth, which is 56 yards in length by 45 yards in breadth, an under-water inspection showed that it is composed of beams and stones intermingled.

At the south-west end of Loch Ness, and about 150 yards from the shore, there is situated the only island in the loch. It is oval-shaped, and before the raising of the level of the water was about 60 yards long by 56 yards broad. To see whether it might possibly be a crannog, Mr. Blundell made several descents in the diving dress, and discovered that at the junction of the sloping sides with the loch floor a wooden framework or platform ran in below the rubble building, and therefore that this immense mass, the diameter of which at the bottom is about 100 yards, must have been originally constructed on the surface and sunk into its present position. One of the islands on Loch Moy, near Inverness, has been partially examined by the same investigator. In spite of its great size (about two acres superficial), he is of opinion that it will likely turn out to be an artificial construction.

Lastly, the island on the Loch of Leys, near Banchory, now dry land, may be mentioned. When the loch was drained sixty years ago, Sir James Burnett of Crathes made an examination of this crannog, but unfortunately the printed account is rather meagre. It was about 70 yards long by 34 yards broad, and as usual was distant about 100 yards from the nearest point of the mainland. On reaching the foundation, the explorers found that the lowest stratum of the island was composed of logs of oak and birch, upon which layers of mixed material had been accumulated.

In view of these facts it would be rash to exclude the possibility of the Castle Island being a crannog. Some significance also should be attached to the large number of oak beams which have been from time to time fished up, especially from between the island and the north shore (see pp. 82-9). Submerged gangways fixed to the bottom between the crannogs and the land are a constant feature of our lake-dwellings. Why they should have been submerged has not been very clearly explained, but they are so often present that they must have served some purpose. The planks and beams recovered in such abundance at the Castle Island have generally been accepted as part of the bridge which formerly crossed the north channel, and it is no doubt correct that many of them had belonged to this comparatively modern structure. But the unanimity with which all the old accounts speak of the wood-work as having been dragged up from the *bottom* is highly suspicious, and suggests that we have here to do rather with a prehistoric submerged gangway than with the timbers of a mediaeval or modern bridge, the under-water parts of which would have consisted for the most part of round piles. As Dr. Munro remarks, the fishing up of oak beams from the bottom of a lake or their discovery under its surface inextricably mortised into others, as some of them were at Kinnord, is regarded as evidence for the existence of a crannog. At p. 87 it will be seen that Mr. Michie had detected the peculiar character of some of the logs recovered, and found it impossible to believe that they had formed part of the framework of the bridge.

In order to obtain direct proof one way or another as to the true nature of the island, it was thought that the water telescope might be useful, and Mr. Walker, School of Glen Tanar, was kind enough to undertake an examination of the sides and bottom from a boat with this instrument. The results, however, were negative. No wood-work was observed, and, where the sides could be seen through the weeds and grasses, no evidence of artificiality could be detected; but on the other hand the general under-water appearance of the Prison Island (undoubtedly artificial) was not materially dissimilar. Hence the conclusion, that only by excavation is a final decision possible.

Whether the big island is artificial or not, the arrangement of crannogs in pairs is a common feature in many lochs. Loch Moy, mentioned above, presents an exact parallel to Loch Kinnord. On it there are two islands, one large and probably a crannog; the other, 100 yards off, much smaller and certainly so, and curiously enough also said to have been a prison. Again, in the loch of Forfar, the island known as Queen Margaret's Inch was about the same size as the Castle Island, and was partly, if not more probably altogether, artificial. Associated with it was a small crannog. Other examples of the same arrangement could be given. This conjunction of two islands - one large and one small - can hardly be accidental, but probably indicates some purpose of which we are ignorant.

Recent Excavations At Kinnord

The interest with which such Early Celtic lake-dwellings as we have been describing cannot fail to be regarded, is enhanced in the case of Loch Kinnord by the fact that around its shores are still to be seen the remains of the land habitations of the island builders. At pp. 16-24 their position and extent are indicated, and again in the article on Mulloch (pp. 133-140) attention is called to some others in the near neighbourhood. A full account of the exploration of parts of these ruins, carried on by Mr. John Abercromby, will be found in the *Proceedings of the Society of Antiquaries of Scotland*, vol. 38. The following is a short summary of his most important discoveries.

Six circular enclosures were subjected to complete or partial examination. Five of these are situated on the Davan slope of the neck of land between the two lochs, and one a mile further west towards Culblean. Nothing seems to have been attempted at Mr. Michie's groups II and III near New Kinnord, which he describes as being by far the largest, so that future investigators have plenty of virgin ground waiting them there and at Knockice and Mulloch. The walls of the enclosures, which are in some cases over 12 feet in thickness, were found to be constructed on the principle of laying two rows of large stones to form the outer and inner faces respectively, and filling up the intervening space with smaller stones. Where the structure was not greatly dilapidated, the foundations were seen to be well and firmly laid, embedded a considerable distance in the subsoil. Some of the stones are of such a size that several men must have been needed to place them in position. One of the enclosures had its whole interior area paved with large blocks, many of them of very regular quadrangular form. In the Culblean enclosure there is at one point a curious arrangement in the wall, which in other respects presents no special feature. Three very large stones are so arranged as to form a quadrangular orifice about 2 feet wide by 1 foot high, and 2 feet deep horizontally; the whole has something of the appearance of a huge open-air ambry. Mr. Abercromby says that a careful examination failed to reveal what this construction could have been intended for.

The whole interior of at least one of the enclosures was trenched down to the natural "pan"; in others trenches were run across. The material was riddled and careful watch kept for relics of human manufacture or other evidences of human occupation. The finds were extremely few, though of course in dealing with circles as large as 20 yards in diameter it is quite possible that some objects may have escaped observation. The list consisted of pieces of flint flake, showing signs of use; a flint arrow-head; some fragments of glazed pottery, wheel-made, which from their position are quite possibly modern; a stone disc, 4 inches in diameter and $1\frac{1}{2}$ inches thick, resembling those found at the Culbin sands, the purpose of which is unknown; and a number of pieces of charcoal. In one of the enclosures a layer of charcoal, 2 feet square, was noticed at a depth of 1 foot, and below this two other layers of the same nature; patches of burnt earth and ashes were also found. These no doubt mark the sites of hearths and fireplaces.

The archaeological remains, it will thus be seen, were not sufficient to determine the use to which these enclosures were put. Mr. Abercromby's conclusion that some of them at least may have been meant for cattle-pens agrees with that of Mr. Michie given on p. 140. The long lines of stones, leading between the enclosures, called by Mr. Michie "walled roads," remain an unsolved problem. Their chief peculiarity is "the constant small changes in the direction of their alignment," and the occurrence of great blocks at intervals among the smaller stones.

If the crop of relics was distinctly disappointing, the explorers had the satisfaction of revealing the existence of two underground houses among the ruins. Both lie near Loch Davan. The second was only noticed on the last day of the investigations, when no time remained to clear it out. It lies close to and outside one of the circles, and was discovered, when a trench was sunk across a hollow, which, it was suspected, might mark the site of an earth-house. At a depth of $7\frac{1}{2}$ feet a "fine piece of smooth, well-laid pavement, 5 feet 10 inches wide," was struck. A few pieces of charcoal, and particles of bone were brought to light. Nothing further was done to lay the structure bare, and the trench was filled up and returfed, to await some future explorer.

A fairly complete examination was made of the other. It also lies near the same enclosure, but on the south and opposite side and adjoining a low circular mound bounded by a ring of large stones placed at intervals, about 20 yards in diameter. This earth-house exhibits the usual structural features of the peculiar class of buildings to which it belongs. The entrance, which is at the surface level, is marked by two large stones, one on each side, and presents the appearance of a narrow passage, a few feet wide. The bottom is a well-laid pavement, and after entrance the sides are seen to be formed of very large stones, carefully placed so as to present a smooth surface. The passage begins to sink immediately after the opening till the floor is about 6 feet below the level of the ground. The total length is 41 feet. As usual in such buildings, the direction changes at some distance from the door, though in this case the curvature is slighter than in most examples, and towards the end the chamber expands into a pear-shaped bulb. The roof had evidently been of wood, as no covering slabs were to be seen. Though none of the relics recovered were very striking, there was abundant evidence of human occupation, such as pieces of charcoal and burnt bones, stones blackened by fire, and layers of black ashes, part of a burnt hazel nut, the upper stone of a quern, and an angular piece of iron. From the last two objects the deduction can be made that the inhabitants of the earth-house were agriculturists as well as hunters, and that the period of occupation lasted as late as the Iron Age. This conclusion agrees with the results arrived at regarding all the earth-houses in Scotland which have yielded relics or other evidence by which their date may be determined. Their archaeological remains are similar to those found in crannogs, and there is general agreement that chronologically they are to be taken together. Both were evidently in use down to Roman times, as objects of Roman origin have been found in both. For example, in an earth-house at Castle Newe, Strathdon, a coin of the emperor Nerva (A.D. 96-98) was picked up, and in one at Crichton, Midlothian, some of the stones used to form the walls showed ornamentation which indicated that they had originally formed part of a Roman building.

The most important discovery in connection with the Kinnord earth-house related, not to its relics, but to its position with regard to the contiguous buildings, a discovery which helps to clear up the whole problem of underground dwellings and their purpose. On emerging from the chamber the observer finds himself within a circular enclosure, about 20 yards in diameter, round the circumference of which is a ring of stones placed at intervals. The floor of this enclosure was found to consist of a pavement, *which is continuous with the pavement of the earth-house*. At many points traces of fire and charcoal were noticed. The conclusion seems certain that, within this circle, the inhabitants of the underground dwelling had their overground houses which, being of wood, have of course totally disappeared. Touching the circle is another, already mentioned; it is unpaved and may have been used as a cattle-pen.

The same association of underground with overground

dwellings is seen in the Milton of Whitehouse earth-house, four miles north of Kinnord, discovered and excavated in 1894 (see figs., pp. 24-5). In this case a sandy hillock had been selected for the site, probably on account of its dryness. It differs from the Kinnord example principally in the sharp curvature at D ; most of the other features are the same. From A to G internally the distance is 37 feet 6 inches; about 9 feet of the floor at the inner end is paved, and at G there are some flat stones which seem meant to form a seat. At H and I there are stone pillars, probably parts of the original doors, which would have been of wood; in some earth-houses the door checks are at the sides of the passage. No roofing stones were found, either in position or in the interior of the chamber, so that here, as at Kinnord, wood must have been the material employed. Very few articles of human use were noted - a piece of bronze wire looped at one end which looked like a brooch pin, a stone whorl, and fragments of querns and clay vessels. But there were quantities of ashes and charred wood. Before the discovery of the house, "large quantities of ashes had been turned up at different times by the plough in a hollow in the field near to the house, where doubtless the original inhabitants had been in the habit of emptying them." At a distance of 18 feet from the entrance there is a piece of pavement, 7 feet 9 inches long and 5 feet 3 inches at the broadest end. It consists of flat, undressed stones, and is raised somewhat above the level of the field. Ashes were found in abundance round it. Here we have, no doubt, the remains of an overground dwelling, the perishable parts of which have disappeared.*

*According to Mr. Michie (in *Scottish Notes and Queries*, 1896) "there are now no fewer than 6 earth-houses within the bounds of

Earth-houses, similar in their most characteristic features to those we have been describing, exist or are known to have once existed in all parts of Scotland, and are especially plentiful in the north-east. In their present condition, any overground buildings which may once have accompanied them have disappeared, either from natural decay or agricultural operations. In fact most of them have been discovered by accident, usually through the plough coming in contact with the slabs of the roof; and thus the most striking peculiarity about them to the modern eye is their secrecy. Hence, no doubt, has arisen the common notion of their purpose, that they were meant for hiding-places where the inhabitants took refuge when unable to resist their enemies in the open, emerging again to an open-air existence when the danger passed. But if the arrangement which we have seen at Kinnord and Milton was general - and there is evidence that it was - these subterranean dwellings could not have been designed for concealment. On the surface beside them and associated with them were other houses, cattle-folds, and buildings of various kinds. Once an enemy was in possession of these, he could not miss the earth-houses, more especially as the arrangement of buildings in his own village would be just the same. Besides, it would be difficult to imagine a worse defensive device than an earth-house; in the event of discovery, the fugitives could be comfortably destroyed at leisure.

Cromar in some state of preservation, besides many that have been demolished before their significance was known, *viz.*, 2 at Culsh, 2 at Crossfold, 1 at Migvie (the ruins of another were found here), and 1 at Milton. A large one was discovered on the farm of Groddie, but being in the middle of an arable field has been filled up and obliterated."

It is much more likely that these souterrains were used for domestic purposes, as adjuncts of ordinary surface dwellings, though what the supposed advantages which led to their construction may have been it might be hard to say. The example described at p. 96 is one of the most curious, both from the bifurcation at the end and from the low height of the roof, 16 to 30 inches; it could hardly have been used as a living chamber.

In another respect, too, the present aspect of our earth-houses is apt to be misleading. With their dismal and uncomfortable appearance, especially when the original roof is in position, they look like the retreats of some race of barbarous troglodytes. The archaeological remains, however, which they yield, will speedily dispose of such an idea, even if it were not known to be mistaken on other grounds. The following finds have been recorded from

FIG. 21. - BRONZE ARMLET FOUND IN EARTH-HOUSE AT CASTLE NEWE, STRATHDON.
FRONT VIEW.

underground dwellings in various parts of Scotland:- bones of wild animals, but also those of the ox, horse, sheep, dog, and domestic fowl, in abundance; querns (in one souterrain no fewer than 10 were found); objects of iron, which, owing to oxidisation, are mostly difficult to identify, but in one case the article seemed to be part of a spade; staves of a cog of wood and a comb of the same material; spindle whorls of stone and one of lead; various stone vessels, some of them apparently lamps; bronze needles and pins; bone buttons; coarse handmade pottery, but also the wheel-made variety, and fragments of lustrous ware commonly called Samian; beads of vitreous paste, of various shapes and colours; bronze articles for wearing on the person, especially massive armlets. A pair of these were discovered at the entrance to an earth-house at Castle Newe, Strathdon (see figs. 21-22). They are $5\frac{3}{4}$ inches in diameter and are formed of cast metal; the circular spaces at the extremities are filled with enamels of chequered pattern in red and yellow. Similar to these, but of a slightly different design, are the specimens found near an earth-house at Crossfold, Coull (see pp. 138-9); in the

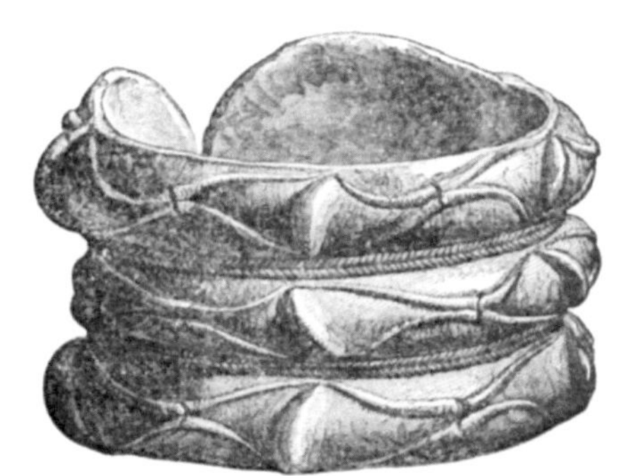

FIG. 22. - BRONZE ARMLET.
BACK VIEW.

latter, the enamels, which no doubt originally occupied the circular spaces, are wanting.

Though from these data a complete picture of the life of the earth-house builders cannot be reconstructed, the degree of civilisation to which they had attained is indicated clearly enough in a general way. They lived partly by the chase, but they also tilled the ground and grew grain, querns being commoner than any other class of relic in the houses. They reared domestic animals; spun and wove cloth and sewed it into clothing; manufactured pottery at home, but also, as the Samian ware shows, traded for it and other articles, with the parts of Britain to the south occupied by the Romans. With the manipulation of metals they were thoroughly at home; they used iron for their cutting weapons and some of their implements, while still retaining bronze (the older metal) for other articles and especially for ornamental purposes. Their mechanical skill in works on a large scale has already been remarked upon in connection with the crannogs; and from the smaller archaeological remains, such as the armlets and similar objects, they can be seen to have possessed a high degree of taste and manipulative dexterity. One might be tempted to explain the occurrence in rude earth-houses of articles so artistically fashioned by regarding them as imported, and not native productions; but this cannot have been the case, because the stone moulds, not perhaps of these very armlets but of metal-work of a similar character, have been found in various parts of Scotland, as far north as Shetland,

In view of all these facts, it seems possible to believe, without reading into the evidence more than it will bear, that the material civilisation of the earth-house building Picts was not in any very essential respect much inferior to that of their descendants in the early historic period.

THE NAME OF THE LOCH

IT will have been noticed in the course of the book that the name of the loch appears in a variety of forms, of which Kinnord, Kander, and Canmore, with slight modifications in spelling, are the chief. The first, Kinnord or Kinord, may now be said to have ousted the others in writing and in local "polite" speaking, but it is the most recent of the three, and even yet has not quite established itself in genuine native speech in the district.

If a native were asked to name the loch and the places round it according to familiar and unsophisticated usage, the following would be his nomenclature:- the farm on the north shore he would call Kinnord; the farms on the south and east he would call the Muckle Kenner and the Little Kenner respectively; and the loch itself, Loch Kenner. (In Kinnord the accent is on the second syllable, in Kenner on the first). A good local authority writes: "More than fifty years ago, Kenner was the usual name, but old people sometimes said Kanner. The loch and the farm, now written Meikle Kinnord, were called Kenner; Kinnord applied only to the farm between the two lochs; the expression Loch Kinnord was never heard among the common people."

That this is the historical usage is confirmed by

documentary evidence. One or two references, among many that might be given, will suffice to show it. In the Parochial Registers of Glenmuick in 1775 "Mr. McInnes, Kinord," is followed in the next line by "Donald Simpson, Kander," these being the north and south farms respectively. In the Poll Book (1696) the same distinction is seen. James Man in 1753 says "the inhabitants call it Loch Keandor, on the side of which there is a farm called Kean-ord." In 1679 we have (Ant. of Abd. and Banff, III, 287), "the loch and lands of Kandar(s)." The Act of Parliament of 1648 (see p. 81) calls the loch Kender.

Clearly, therefore, we have to do with two names, (1) Kinnord, for the north farm, and (2) Kander, or Kanner, or Kenner for the loch and the other two farms. If any doubt remains, direct proof is forthcoming from the practice of Gaelic speakers further west, in Braemar, *where the true Gaelic forms of the names can still be heard*. In Gaelic, Kinnord is *Ceann nan ord* and the name applies only to the north farm; the loch itself is *Ceanndair*.

As regards the etymology and meaning of these words the first is simple. Ceann means a head; and ord, a hammer, is common in place-names as applied to hills, more especially those of a rounded, hammer shape, but often to eminences generally. Thus the meaning of *Ceann nan ord* is "head, or end, of the heights," In looking for the heights, we must remember that the name properly belongs to the place at the west end of the elevated ridge between the two lochs, not to the present New Kinnord. East of this ridge again we have the Ordie, which no doubt represents G. Ordaidh (dh silent), a derivative of Ord. The Ords, therefore, referred to in Ceann nan ord, are pretty obviously these two ridges. (This does not exhaust all the instances of *ord* in the district. South of the loch we have the well-defined, hammer-shaped hill, so called; and on the slope of Culblean, to the west of the Ballater-Coldstone road, there are the Muckle Ord and the Little Ord, both rounded eminences).

Ceanndair, as we have seen, applies both to the loch and to the farms on its south and east shores. Presumably it is originally a loch name, the farms being called from it and not vice versa. The derivation of the word shows that this is so. Its elements are *ceann*, head, and *dobhar*, water (bh silent). As ceann is the qualifying term, it bears the accent, and hence the second syllable is reduced to *dair* (der), the whole being pronounced nearly like Kyander in English spelling. The meaning is "head water," or "high water." Considering the situation of the loch, this would seem to indicate that it received its name from the point of view of those who lived further down the valley.

There is a second Loch Kander on Deeside, also called by Gaelic speakers Ceanndair. "Head water" is in this case peculiarly appropriate, for it lies at the head of Glen Callater, more than two thousand feet above sea-level, in as wild a spot as can be seen in the Braemar highlands. Near Taynuilt on the west coast we have a third instance in Barr-cheanndair, "peak of Ceanndair," Ceanndair itself referring to the loch lying below the peak. Loch Kinder, in Kirkcudbrightshire, is also probably the same word, though of course the living Gaelic is not obtainable in this case to prove it.

Parallel to Ceanndair, both in formation and meaning, is Aber-*ardour* in Crathie, which also occurs elsewhere in

Scotland. In Gaelic it is Obair-Ardair, "the mouth of the Ardour." Macbain derives from ard, high, and dobhar, which gives the meaning " high water."

The history of the *Kenner* of popular speech can now be traced step by step from the original *Ceanndair*. When Gaelic became extinct in the district, Ceanndair survived as Kander, and so continued in documents till recently. In colloquial Scots, however, the *d* tended to disappear, just as "wander" becomes "wan'er," "gander" "gan'er," etc. It is worth notice that the *y* sound heard in the Gaelic (Kyander) used to be sometimes heard from old people: they said Kyanner rather than Kanner. The next change was to substitute *e* for *a* in the first syllable under the influence of the *e* in the second (umlaut). Thus: Ceanndair > Kander > Kanner > Kenner.

There remains the form Loch Canmore to be mentioned. It is found in Wyntoun (15th century), and sometimes in official documents, such as retours, for about two hundred years afterwards. The explanation of this name must lie in Malcolm Canmore's reputed connection with the loch and district (see pp. 35-8). It cannot be regarded as a genuine place-name, first, because there is no trace of it in popular speech, which, as we have just seen, is strongly conservative in such matters; and, secondly and decisively, because the Gaelic for the loch knows nothing of "Canmore."

To the question, which will naturally occur, of why and when *Kinnord* came to supplant *Kander* and *Kenner*, the answer is simple. It is a piece of mistaken refinement. The change was due to the notion which got abroad among the better sort that Kander was somehow a corruption of

Kinnord - an idea which gradually affixed the stigma of vulgarity to the old name and finally expelled it from "correct" speech and writing. Not long after 1806, the farms hitherto called and written Meikle and Little Kander (Kenner) began to be written M. and L. Kinnord, the real Kinnord on the north side of course retaining its name besides. The change from Kander to Kinnord in the case of the loch was later, and did not take place altogether without protest. One local antiquary, the Rev. James Wattie of Bellastraid, did his best to resist the innovation, and we have noticed that most of the maps continued to give the loch as Kander or Ceander till the middle of the century and later.

It may be worth while to put on record the names of a few places round the loch which are not marked on the Ordnance maps or noted in MacDonald's *Placenames of West Aberdeenshire*, and which, owing to depopulation and change of tenancies, may come to be forgotten altogether. The etymologies which are offered for them, it should be noticed, stand on a different footing from those of Kinnord and Kander given above. The following names, being those of small places, are not known in Braemar; and hence, in the absence of the true Gaelic forms, the derivations have not the same certainty.

On the north shore, the narrow flat between the height and the water's edge is called *Rinyach*. The first syllable is *roinn*, a point, or piece of land running to a point; the second is probably *each*, horse. Of old, horses and cattle were pastured separately.

The Cray-ellan. In the north-west corner of the loch there is a small peninsula so called. Up till the middle of last century, when the water-level was lowered, it was an island, as the second syllable shows, G. eilean. Cray probably is from G. cro or cri, a wattled enclosure or sheep-fold, also a cruive. Either meaning might suit here. There may have been some arrangement for catching fish at the place, or it may have been used as a fold, being near the shore and safe. As the accent is on the second syllable in Scots, it probably was the same in Gaelic; hence the meaning is "the island sheep-fold" or "the island cruive," not "the sheep-fold island, the cruive island." On the whole the meaning of sheep-fold is more likely than cruive.

We have the same word in *Cromar*, the Gaelic of which is at the present moment Cro-Mhar, "sheep-fold of Mar," a metaphorical extension which suits the district admirably, encircled as the whole basin is with hills. In Chapel of Garioch there is Crayfold (MacDonald, p. 140), which is obviously a doublet, the second syllable translating the first.

The same rage for correctness, which has tabooed Kander and Kenner, has also turned Cray-ellan into Crow's Island in polite language!

Tominummer, a hillock near the west shore. Probably *Tom an iomair*, "the hillock of the rig" (of land). The popular derivation is that one "Tammie" was in the way of "nummering" his sheep in an adjacent hollow!

Kinnagarry, an old holding, now part of Meikle Kinnord. It lay west of the present farm-house. Perhaps the Gaelic word here is garadh, den, referring to the "glack" at the place. "Denhead."

Carlochy, beside Meikle Kinnord, at the loch side. The long *o* points to Cathair lochaidh (th and dh silent), "black bog." It is low-lying and was boggy at one time.

Presscow. The ruins of this holding are on the east shoulder of the Ord. The first part is of course *preas*, a bush or clump. The old Gaelic *coll*, hazel, regularly becomes in Scots *cow*. Thus Cowie is for *Collaidh,* place of hazels; cp. Towie, older Tolly, G. Tollaidh, from toll, "hole." (Similarly roll, boll etc., become row, bow, in the vernacular). Presscow is thus "hazel clump"; and hazels are still growing plentifully there.

INDEX

MANSE OF DINNET